Walch Hands-on Science Series

Our Solar System

Steven Souza, Ph.D.
and
Karen Kwitter, Ph.D.
Williams College
Williamstown, MA

illustrated by Lloyd Birmingham

Project Editors: Joel Beller and Carl Raab

WALCH PUBLISHING®

Acknowledgment

The authors are grateful for the love and support of their parents: Arthur and Sonia Kwitter, and Manuel and Barbara Souza.

The authors thank their sons Randy and Aaron for their encouragement and for trying out some of these activities.

User's Guide
to
Walch Reproducible Books

As part of our general effort to provide educational materials that are as practical and economical as possible, we have designated this publication a "reproducible book." The designation means that purchase of the book includes purchase of the right to limited reproduction of all pages on which this symbol appears:

Here is the basic Walch policy: We grant to individual purchasers of this book the right to make sufficient copies of reproducible pages for use by all students of a single teacher. This permission is limited to a single teacher and does not apply to entire schools or school systems, so institutions purchasing the book should pass the permission on to a single teacher. Copying of the book or its parts for resale is prohibited.

Any questions regarding this policy or requests to purchase further reproduction rights should be addressed to:

Permissions Editor
J. Weston Walch, Publisher
P.O. Box 658
Portland, Maine 04104-0658

☀ Contents

☀ To the Teacher

This is one in a series of hands-on science activity books for middle school and early high school students. A recent national survey of middle school students conducted by the National Science Foundation (NSF) found that

- more than half listed science as their favorite subject.
- more than half wanted more hands-on activities.
- 90 percent stated the best way for them to learn science was to do experiments themselves.

The books in this series seek to capitalize on that NSF survey. The books are not texts but supplements, written by teachers. They offer hands-on, fun activities that will turn some students on to science. You and your students should select which activities are to be carried out. All of the activities need not be done. Pick and choose those activities that best meet the needs of your students. All of these activities can be done in school, and some can be done at home.

Students will need only basic, standard scientific equipment or household items that can be found in most middle and high school science laboratories or homes. The activities range from the simple (drawing ellipses to represent planetary orbits) to the difficult (observing the Sun). There is something for every student.

THE ACTIVITIES CAN BE USED:

- to provide hands-on experiences pertaining to textbook content.
- to reinforce key scientific principles through direct experience.
- to give verbally limited children a chance to succeed and gain extra credit.
- as the basis for class or school science fair projects or for other science competitions.
- to involve students in science club undertakings.
- as homework assignments.
- to involve parents in their child's science education and experiences.
- to foster an appreciation of the solar system and our place in it.

Students can learn important scientific principles from carrying out these activities. For example:

- The planets move in predictable paths governed by physical laws.
- Many geological features such as impact craters and volcanoes are not unique to Earth, but are found through much of the solar system.
- The compositions of the planets are a result of the way in which the solar system formed.

Each activity has a Teacher Resource section that includes, besides helpful hints and suggestions, a scoring rubric, quiz questions, and Internet connections for those students who wish to go further and carry out the follow-up activities. Instructional objectives and the National Science Standards that apply to each activity are provided to help you meet state and local expectations.

The Scale of the Solar System: How Big Are the Planets?

 INSTRUCTIONAL OBJECTIVES

Students will be able to

- describe the relative sizes of the planets.
- understand how small the planets are compared with the Sun.

 NATIONAL SCIENCE STANDARDS ADDRESSED

Students demonstrate an understanding of

- Earth in the solar system.

Students demonstrate scientific inquiry and problem-solving skills by

- using evidence from reliable sources to develop models.
- working in teams to collect and share information and ideas.

Students demonstrate effective scientific communication by

- arguing from evidence and data.
- representing data in multiple ways.

 MATERIALS

For each group:

- Model Sun (one for the entire class)
- Objects brought from home or provided by the teacher to represent the planets
- Modeling clay
- Calculator

For Extension:

- Flexible tape measure

HELPFUL HINTS AND DISCUSSION

Time frame: 40 minutes, or a single period
Structure: In groups of two or three students
Location: In class

The goal of this activity is to create a scale model of sizes for the planets and the Sun. This activity should precede the activity entitled "The Scale of the Solar System: How Far Apart Are the Planets?" In that activity, students get to appreciate the vast distances between the major bodies of the solar system.

In this activity, you can prime students for the concept that if the planets are represented by the relative sizes of the objects they assemble here, the scale orbits would have to be extremely large. If the Earth is the size of a green pea, then Pluto's orbit would have to be about 9,000 feet (1.7 miles) from the model Sun. Because of the relative sizes and vast distances between planets, it is difficult to make a scale model of the solar system that is accurate in both size and separation. If the planets are big enough to see, then the orbits have to be tremendous, but if the orbits are small enough to draw on a piece of paper, then the planets are too small to see.

Each group of two or three students will assemble models for all the planets, but there will be just one model Sun for the entire class, which you will provide. The spherical object you choose to represent the Sun will establish the scale for the other solar system objects. The object should be large, to make the scale reasonable, but not so large as to create a hazard in class. Anything from a basketball to a small weather balloon should work. Find the scale in units of inches (or cm) per Earth diameter. If you use a beach ball 1 foot in diameter to represent the Sun, then the scale would be 0.1 inch per Earth diameter. Jupiter could be a candy jawbreaker about 1.25 inches in diameter. Ask the students to bring to class items that can serve as models for the planets. Since they won't know the scale ahead of time, students should be encouraged to bring small spherical items in a wide range of sizes, from a grain of sand to a baseball. (If you find a model "Sun" bigger than 30 inches in diameter, they will need something larger than a baseball to be "Jupiter.") Dried peas, peppercorns, pebbles, marbles, Ping-Pong balls, etc., are good suggestions. Show the model Sun to the class and tell them what the scale will be in inches or centimeters per Earth diameter at the beginning of the activity. Modeling clay (to make model planets) and/or a selection of other objects (like ball bearings) can be made available to supplement what the students bring in.

ADAPTATIONS FOR HIGH AND LOW ACHIEVERS

High Achievers: Encourage these students to do the Extension and Follow-up Activity.

Low Achievers: Have reference books available for these students. Review the concept of a scale model, and how to construct one.

SCORING RUBRIC

Full credit can be given to students who fill in Table 2 reasonably and make a reasonable scale model of the planets. Extra credit can be given to students who do the Extensions or Follow-up Activity. The quiz can be scored from 1 to 4 correct.

INTERNET TIE-INS   http://pds.jpl.nasa.gov/planets/

QUIZ
1. The two largest planets are _____ and _____.
2. Which is the smallest planet?
3. Why are the outer planets (except Pluto) larger than the inner planets?
4. True or False: There are as many planets in our solar system that are larger than Earth as there are planets that are smaller.

Name _____ Date _____

The Scale of the Solar System: How Big Are the Planets?

☼ BEFORE YOU BEGIN ☼

The Earth seems very large to someone standing on it. Yet, Earth is among the smaller planets in our solar system, all dwarfed by the immense Sun. Table 1 below lists the diameters of the planets relative to Earth's diameter. As you can see, even Jupiter, the largest planet, is only about one tenth the Sun's diameter. And Pluto, the smallest planet, is almost 600 times smaller than the Sun.

Conditions and processes that were at work during the formation of the solar system about 5 billion years ago created the planets that we now see. As you will learn, the next four planets beyond Mars contain enormous amounts of the very light gases hydrogen and helium. These gases, which Mercury, Venus, Earth, and Mars do not contain much of, make Jupiter, Saturn, Uranus, and Neptune very large. In this activity you will create a scale model of the planets and see their relative sizes.

Table 1. Relative Diameters

Planet	Diameter (Earth diameters)
Mercury	0.38
Venus	0.95
Earth	1.00
Mars	0.53
Jupiter	11.2
Saturn	9.5
Uranus	4.0
Neptune	3.9
Pluto	0.19
Sun	**110**

MATERIALS

- Model Sun (one for the entire class)
- Objects brought from home or provided by the teacher to represent the planets
- Modeling clay

- Calculator

EXTENSION

- Flexible tape measure

PROCEDURE

1. At the beginning of this exercise your teacher will show you an object that will represent the Sun, and will tell you the scale you will use in either cm or inches. On this scale, in cm or inches, the Earth's diameter will be assigned 1 unit, and the other solar system objects will be proportional to Earth. For example, if your scale has Earth's diameter as 2 cm, then Mercury's diameter, which is 0.38 × Earth's, would be 0.38 × 2 cm = 0.76 cm. Make a note of this scale in the Data Collection and Analysis section. Circle the units you used (**in.** or **cm**).

(continued)

How Big Are the Planets? *(continued)*

2. For each planet, and for the Sun, calculate the scale model size in inches or cm by multiplying each body's relative size (given in Table 1) by the scale you have written in the Data Collection and Analysis section. Write your values in Table 2 in the Data Collection and Analysis section. Circle the units you used (**in.** or **cm**).

3. Compare your results with the other members of your group and make corrections if any of your answers are very different from the others'.

Do steps 4 and 5 with your entire group.

4. For each planet, find or make an object with the required diameter. If no object with the proper size was brought to class, make a ball of clay of the right size.

5. Bring your collection of planets near the model Sun. Each member of your group should make a sketch of the planets and Sun together.

EXTENSION

Measure the circumference of the model Sun and calculate its diameter. Use the formula $D = C/\pi$, where D is the diameter and C is the circumference. Write your answer in the Data Collection and Analysis section below Table 2.

DATA COLLECTION AND ANALYSIS

Scale: _____ (in or cm)/Earth diameter

Table 2. Scale Model Sizes

Planet	Scale Model Diameter (in. or cm)
Mercury	
Venus	
Earth	
Mars	
Jupiter	
Saturn	
Uranus	
Neptune	
Pluto	
Sun	

EXTENSION

Circumference of model Sun: _____ inches or cm

Diameter of model Sun: _____ inches or cm

(continued)

How Big Are the Planets? *(continued)*

❓ CONCLUDING QUESTIONS

1. How many times larger is the diameter of the largest planet than the diameter of the smallest?

   _____

2. Where does Earth fall in the range of planet sizes? _____

3. True or False: Jupiter is nearly as large as the Sun. _____

EXTENSION

Is the value for the Sun's diameter that you got from the circumference the same as the value in Table 2? If not, what might be true about your model planets?

☀ Follow-up Activity ☀

Relative diameters tell you about how big two objects are compared with each other. It is also interesting to know the total **volume** of an object. Calculate the relative volumes of all the planets and the Sun, compared with the Earth. To do this, take the relative diameters given in Table 1 and **cube** them (calculate diameter × diameter × diameter). This gives you the relative volumes. Do your calculations agree with the statement that the Sun contains more than 1 million times as much volume as the Earth?

The Scale of the Solar System: How Far Apart Are the Planets?

 ## INSTRUCTIONAL OBJECTIVES

Students will be able to

- describe the placement of the planets in the solar system.
- define the astronomical unit.
- calculate the separations between the orbits of any two planets.

 ## NATIONAL SCIENCE STANDARDS ADDRESSED

Students demonstrate an understanding of

- Earth's place in the solar system.

Students demonstrate scientific inquiry and problem-solving skills by

- working individually and in teams to collect and share information and ideas.

Students demonstrate effective scientific communication by

- arguing from evidence and data.
- representing data and results in multiple ways.

 ## MATERIALS

Part A

For each pair of students:

- A large sheet of drawing or wrapping paper (about 1 m × 1 m)
- Pencil
- Thick cardboard
- Meterstick
- Drawing compass
- Thumbtack or pushpin
- String or sewing thread
- Scissors
- Calculator

Part B

For the whole class:

- Long rope or string (about 200 feet long)
- Ten 8.5" × 11" sheets of paper
- Writing markers
- Tape measure (as long as possible)
- Playing field, sidewalk, or inside hallway long enough to stretch out the rope
- Model Sun, about 4000 times smaller in diameter than the length of the rope

HELPFUL HINTS AND DISCUSSION

Time frame: Part A—40 minutes, or a single period
Part B—about half a period
Structure: Part A in pairs; Part B as a class activity
Location: Part A in class; Part B outdoors or in a very long hallway

Try to get drawing paper as large as possible so that the students will be able to fit Pluto's orbit on the paper and still distinguish the much smaller orbits of the inner planets. The sheet should be at least 36 inches × 36 inches, but 1 m × 1 m (40 inches × 40 inches) would be better. Review with all students how to apply a scale to a model. With 1 m × 1 m paper size, 1 AU could be equal to 1 cm or ½ inch, and all the planets' orbits will fit nicely on the paper. In any case, you should try this yourself in advance so that you can determine the scale that the students should use. The cardboard backing should be thick enough to prevent the point of the thumbtack or compass from scratching the surface of the table or desk. You can use the side of a packing carton, or several layers of paper tablet backing. This backing is only needed near the center of the paper where the point is, and must be small enough that it does not interfere when the students draw Jupiter's orbit.

For Part B, the list of preparations is included in the Procedure section on the student page. Assign several students to perform each of these tasks. The other students will be "tourists" in the solar system. Students can take turns at planet positions. The rope must be about 200 feet long in order to have a Sun whose scale model size is visible. If you have clothesline rope available, that will do. Several lengths can be tied together if necessary. Otherwise, any strong string will do. The students can use markers to mark the positions of the planets, and then tie labeled tags around the rope. Make sure to stress that even on this 200-foot scale, only the Sun is big enough to be seen from any distance. Jupiter would be the size of a peppercorn, and the other planets would be the size of a grain of sand or smaller.

ADAPTATIONS FOR HIGH AND LOW ACHIEVERS

High Achievers: Encourage these students to do the Extensions and Follow-up Activities.

Low Achievers: Have relevant reference materials available. Review with these students the concept of a scale model, and how to calculate one.

SCORING RUBRIC

Full credit can be given to students whose paper models in Part A are reasonably accurate and who participate appropriately in Part B. The quiz can be scored from 1 to 4 correct. Extra credit can be given to students who do the Extensions or Follow-up Activities.

  INTERNET TIE-INS   http://www.seds.org/nineplanets/nineplanets/overview.html

QUIZ
1. What is an astronomical unit, and how many miles (or km) does it equal?
2. Approximately how many times farther from the Sun is Pluto than Earth?
3. True or False: The planets' orbits are spaced equally outward from the Sun.
4. True or False: The planets are very small compared with the separation between them.

Name _____   Date _____

The Scale of the Solar System: How Far Apart Are the Planets?

☼ BEFORE YOU BEGIN ☼

The solar system is vast. With all the planets, moons, comets, and asteroids you are learning about, it may seem pretty crowded. But space in the solar system is surprisingly empty. Planets, which are the largest bodies orbiting the Sun, are tiny compared with the Sun itself. The distances between the planets are immensely larger than the planets themselves. You may know that the Earth orbits the Sun at an average distance of 93 million miles (150 million km). This distance is called an **astronomical unit**, or 1 AU. But do you know how far Mars is from the Sun? Or Neptune? Table 1 below lists the average distance of each planet from the Sun in AU. In this activity you will see for yourself how widely separated the planets are.

Table 1

Planet	Average Distance from the Sun in AU
Mercury	0.38
Venus	0.72
Earth	**1.00**
Mars	1.52
Jupiter	5.2
Saturn	9.5
Uranus	19.2
Neptune	30.0
Pluto	39.5

 MATERIALS

Part A

For each pair of students:

- A large sheet of drawing or wrapping paper (about 1 m × 1 m)
- Pencil
- Thick cardboard
- Meterstick
- Drawing compass
- Thumbtack or pushpin
- String or sewing thread
- Scissors
- Calculator

Part B

For the whole class:

- Long rope or string (about 200 feet long)
- Ten 8.5" × 11" sheets of paper
- Writing markers
- Tape measure (as long as possible)
- Playing field, sidewalk, or inside hallway long enough to stretch out the rope
- Model Sun, about 4000 times smaller in diameter than the length of the rope

(continued)

How Far Apart Are the Planets? *(continued)*

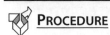 **PROCEDURE**

Part A

In this part of the activity, you will draw the planets' orbits to scale. The orbits of the planets are not exact circles, but in this case, circles will do fine.

1. Using the meterstick, find the center of your sheet of paper. Draw a very small dot in the center of the paper to represent the Sun.

2. Your teacher will give you the scale for determining how large to draw each planet's orbit. Find the radius of each scale orbit by multiplying the true radius in AU from Table 1 by the scale your teacher gives you. This scale will be in either cm/AU or in/AU. Enter your results in Table 2 in the Data Collection and Analysis section.

3. For Mercury, Venus, Earth, and Mars, use the drawing compass to make circles of the proper radius on the paper. Open the compass to the length you calculated for each orbit. Then draw that orbit, centered on the dot representing the Sun.

4. For the remaining planets, you will draw the orbits using a loop of string as a guide. Cut lengths of string for each planet's orbit. Remember that to make a loop, you will need to cut each piece of string *twice* as long as the radius of the orbit you want (plus a little more to allow tying). Then tie the ends of each piece of string together to make a loop.

5. Cut the cardboard into a circle about 5 cm in diameter, and place it underneath the paper, centered on the dot in the center of the paper. The cardboard will keep the thumbtack from tearing the paper or scratching the desk. Insert the thumbtack or pushpin through the paper into the cardboard at the Sun's position. For each planet in turn, starting with Jupiter, place its loop over the thumbtack. Hold the pencil in the loop and, keeping the string taut, draw a circle to represent the orbit, as in Figure 1.

6. Write each planet's name on its proper orbit. Note that on the scale of your drawing the Sun is too small to draw!

EXTENSION

Look up the location of the asteroid belt and include it on your drawing.

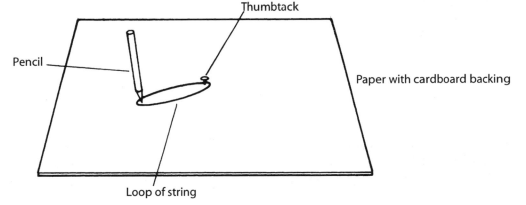

Figure 1

Thumbtack

Pencil

Paper with cardboard backing

Loop of string

(continued)

How Far Apart Are the Planets? *(continued)*

Part B—A Whole-Class Activity

Here are the things that need to be done for this activity. Your teacher may assign you to a specific task.

1. Using the tape measure, measure the full length of the rope. Record this value in the Data Collection and Analysis section. You may have to count several full lengths of the tape measure, plus some additional distance.

2. Establish a scale so that all the planets' orbits will fit somewhere along the rope's length. Record this value above Table 3 in the Data Collection and Analysis section. Determine the scale distance from the Sun to each planet along the rope. Record these values in the Data Collection and Analysis section.

3. Take the rope to the selected location, stretch it out completely, and lay it down on the floor or ground. Decide which end of the rope will represent the Sun. One student should stand at this spot holding the model Sun.

4. Using the distances you calculated in Step 2, measure out from the Sun and mark the position of each planet's orbit. Using a separate sheet of paper for each planet, write the planet's name in large letters with a marker.

5. At each planet's distance along the rope, one student should stand next to the rope and hold up the sheet of paper with the appropriate planet's name on it.

   Once this "solar system" is set up, each student should do the following:

6. Walk the entire length of the rope. Note especially the separations between the planets. Write your observations in the Data Collection and Analysis section.

DATA COLLECTION AND ANALYSIS

Part A

Fill in the scale you used to construct your paper model of the solar system.

1 AU = _____ cm (or _____ in.). Circle either **cm** or **in.** in the table below and enter your values in those units.

Table 2

Planet	Scale Model Distance from the Sun (cm or in.)
Mercury	
Venus	
Earth	
Mars	
Jupiter	
Saturn	
Uranus	
Neptune	
Pluto	

(continued)

How Far Apart Are the Planets? *(continued)*

Part B

Full length of the rope: _____ m, or _____ ft

Fill in the scale you used to construct your rope model of the solar system.

1 AU = _____ m (or _____ ft). Circle either **m** or **ft** in the table below and enter your values in those units.

Table 3

Planet	Scale Model Distance from the Sun (m or ft)
Mercury	
Venus	
Earth	
Mars	
Jupiter	
Saturn	
Uranus	
Neptune	
Pluto	

Observations (from walking the full length of the rope): _____

_____

_____

_____

EXTENSION

Look up the sizes of the planets in a textbook or on the Web. Calculate the size that each planet would be on (1) the scale of your paper model from Part A and (2) the rope model in Part B.

? CONCLUDING QUESTIONS

1. Describe any trend you notice concerning the separations between orbits of planets as you move outward from the Sun.

2. What can you conclude in general about how the size of a planet is related to its distance from the Sun?

(continued)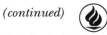

How Far Apart Are the Planets? *(continued)*

☀ Follow-up Activities ☀

1. Make a "solar system map." Obtain a map of your local area showing individual streets and including your school. Pick an interesting point near the edge of the map to represent the Sun. (Your school would be an ideal "Sun.") Establish an appropriate scale, something like 1 cm = 1 AU, depending on the actual size of the map, so that you can fit all the planets' orbits on the map. Draw a circle (or as much of a circle as will fit on the map) representing each planet's orbit at the appropriate distance from the "Sun." Mount your "solar system map" on cardboard and have the students in your class find and label their addresses on it to show which planet orbits nearest their home.

2. Imagine you have a rocket capable of traveling at 50,000 km/hr. Pick any two planets and calculate how long it would take you to get from the first planet's orbit to the second planet's orbit. How long would that same trip take if you traveled in a high-powered race car whose top speed is about 300 km/hr?

Kepler's First Law: Elliptical Orbits

 INSTRUCTIONAL OBJECTIVES

Students will be able to
- identify planetary orbits as ellipses.
- construct an ellipse.

 NATIONAL SCIENCE STANDARDS ADDRESSED

Students demonstrate an understanding of
- predictable motion of the planets.

Students demonstrate scientific inquiry and problem-solving skills by
- identifying variables in experimental and non-experimental settings.

Students demonstrate effective scientific communication by
- representing data in multiple ways.
- arguing from evidence and data.

 MATERIALS

For each student:
- A large piece of drawing paper (about 24" × 24")
- String or strong thread, about 30 inches long
- Scissors
- Colored pencils
- Thumbtacks
- Cardboard backing as big as the drawing paper
- Ruler

HELPFUL HINTS AND DISCUSSION

Time frame: 40 minutes, or a single period
Structure: Individually
Location: In class

Kepler's Laws laid the foundation for Isaac Newton's exploration of orbital motion and gravity in general. Kepler was one of the "giants" on whose shoulders Newton figuratively stood, enabling Newton to make his great contributions to physics. Understanding Kepler's Laws is fundamental to understanding how the solar system works. Kepler's Laws also apply to the motions of double stars orbiting each other, and even to whole galaxies orbiting in space.

Try to get drawing paper that is at least 24 inches × 24 inches, to allow the students to draw several good-sized ellipses. The cardboard backing can be cut from appliance shipping boxes and can be reused many times and shared by several students.

ADAPTATIONS FOR HIGH AND LOW ACHIEVERS

High Achievers: Encourage these students to do the Extensions and Follow-up Activities.

Low Achievers: Have reference material available for consultation. Review the relevant concepts with these students, especially the concept of an ellipse as a geometrical figure.

SCORING RUBRIC

Full credit can be given to students who draw ellipses correctly and who answer the Concluding Questions correctly and in complete sentences. Extra credit can be given to students who complete any of the Extensions or Follow-up Activities. The quiz can be scored from 1 to 4 correct.

 INTERNET TIE-INS   http://windows.ivv.nasa.gov/the_universe/uts/kepler1.html

 QUIZ
1. What kind of motion is described by Kepler's Laws?
2. What is the shape of a planet's orbit around the Sun?
3. Where is the Sun located in that orbit?
4. The longest straight line you can draw across an ellipse is called the _____ axis.

Name _____   Date _____

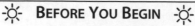

☀ BEFORE YOU BEGIN ☀

It was common knowledge thousands of years ago that several "wandering stars" moved in the sky among the stars of the familiar constellations. Today we know that these wandering objects are the planets. The word **planets** comes from the Greek word, *planetai*, meaning "wanderers." The wandering of these bodies provided evidence that they were not stationary with respect to the stars in the sky, but moved in regular orbits. The first person to correctly describe the motion of the planets around the Sun in mathematical terms was Johannes Kepler. He lived in Germany about 400 years ago. Through painstaking calculations over many years, Kepler discovered three principles, which we call **Kepler's Laws**, that govern how planets move.

Kepler's First Law states that the orbit of a planet around the Sun is an **ellipse**. An ellipse is shown in Figure 1. Notice that an ellipse is a geometrical shape like a flattened circle. The longest straight line you can draw across an ellipse is called the **major axis**, and the distance from the center to one end of the major axis is called the **semimajor axis**. There are two special points that lie along the major axis. Each of these points is called a **focus** of the ellipse. For objects in the solar system, the Sun is at one focus, and the other focus is just empty space. The true orbits of the planets are in fact very close in shape to a circle, which is really a kind of ellipse with only one focus at its center. In this activity, you will examine the properties of an ellipse as described in Kepler's First Law.

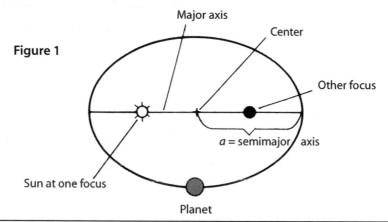

Figure 1

Major axis

Center

Other focus

a = semimajor axis

Sun at one focus

Planet

 MATERIALS

- A large piece of drawing paper (about 24" × 24")
- String or strong thread, about 30 inches long
- Scissors
- Colored pencils
- Thumbtacks
- Cardboard backing as big as the drawing paper
- Ruler

(continued)

Name _____   Date _____

Kepler's First Law: Elliptical Orbits *(continued)*

 <u>**PROCEDURE**</u>

1. Place the cardboard backing under the drawing paper on a flat surface.

2. Near the middle of the paper, press two thumbtacks about 5 inches apart into the paper and backing.

3. Cut the string into one piece about 18 inches long and another about 12 inches long. Tie the ends of each piece together to form two loops.

4. Place the large loop loosely over the thumbtacks.

5. Hold one of the colored pencils straight up inside the loop and stretch the string until it is fairly taut, but not so taut as to dislodge the thumbtacks. Place the pencil point on the paper. Keeping the tension on the string, move the pencil all the way around the thumbtacks, drawing on the paper as you do so, as shown in Figure 2, until you have drawn a complete curve. You have just drawn an ellipse. Label the curve "5."

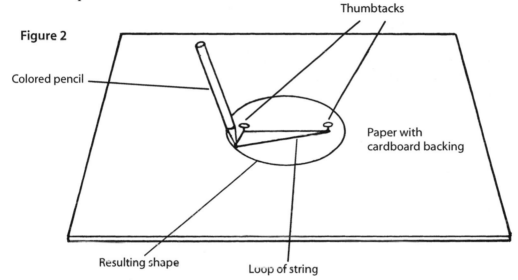

Figure 2

Thumbtacks

Colored pencil

Paper with cardboard backing

Resulting shape

Loop of string

6. Move one of the thumbtacks 2 inches toward the other thumbtack, making them 3 inches apart. Using a different color pencil, repeat step 5. Label the curve "3."

7. Move the same thumbtack as in step 6 back toward its original location, and then out about 2 more inches. The two thumbtacks should now be about 7 inches apart. Using a third color pencil, repeat step 5. Label the curve "7."

8. Put the thumbtack back in its original position (5 inches from the other thumbtack) and remove the large loop. Now place the small loop over the thumbtacks and repeat step 5 with yet another color pencil. Label the curve "5 small."

9. Examine the four figures you have now drawn. Write your description in the Data Collection and Analysis section.

<u>EXTENSION</u>

Turn the paper over. Draw a circle using a single thumbtack and either loop of string. Now compare this procedure with the procedure you used to draw an ellipse. Write your answer in the Data Collection and Analysis section.

(continued)

Kepler's First Law: Elliptical Orbits *(continued)*

 DATA COLLECTION AND ANALYSIS

Compare the shapes of the four figures you have drawn. What do they have in common? What features are different about each of them?

_____

_____

EXTENSION

Comparison of procedures for drawing a circle and an ellipse.

_____

_____

CONCLUDING QUESTIONS

1. Describe two ways to change the shape of an ellipse.

_____

_____

2. What happens to the shape of an ellipse when the two focus points are moved farther apart while the size of the loop is held constant?

_____

_____

3. What happens to the shape of an ellipse when the focus points are held constant but the size of the loop is increased?

_____

_____

EXTENSION

Compare a circle and an ellipse in the following way. A circle represents all points that are a given distance (one radius) away from the center of the circle. Now think about how you drew an ellipse. Can you come up with a description of an ellipse that is similar to this description of a circle?

☼ Follow-up Activities ☼

1. Johannes Kepler's life (1571–1630) was an interesting one. He lived during the turbulent Thirty Years War in Europe and his mother was once put on trial for witchcraft! Write a brief report on Kepler's life using resources in the library and on the World Wide Web.

2. Look up more information about ellipses in a geometry book. Make a poster describing the properties of ellipses and present it to the class.

INSTRUCTIONAL OBJECTIVES

Students will be able to

- state Kepler's Second Law.
- describe how a planet changes speed as it moves in an elliptical orbit.

 NATIONAL SCIENCE STANDARDS ADDRESSED

Students demonstrate an understanding of

- predictable motion of the planets.

Students demonstrate scientific inquiry and problem-solving skills by

- identifying variables in experimental and non-experimental settings.
- working in groups to collect and share information and ideas.

Students demonstrate effective scientific communication by

- representing data in multiple ways.
- arguing from evidence and data.

 MATERIALS

For each pair of students:

- Pen or pencil
- Calculator
- Protractor
- Ruler
- Access to a photocopier

HELPFUL HINTS AND DISCUSSION

Time frame:	40 minutes, or a single period
Structure:	In pairs
Location:	In class

It would be helpful for the students to do the activity on Kepler's First Law before they do this activity. That way, they would already be familiar with the concept that planetary orbits are ellipses, and they will have had a chance to draw and examine ellipses.

The procedure calls for both students in a pair to work together to draw the sectors of the orbit on Figure 2, but then to count squares and measure arcs separately working from photocopies of their work in steps 1–4. If a photocopier is not available for this purpose, have the students in a pair each work on their own copy of Figure 2, helping each other through steps 1–4 but working separately on the remainder of the activity.

ADAPTATIONS FOR HIGH AND LOW ACHIEVERS

High Achievers: Encourage these students to do the Extensions and Follow-up Activities.

Low Achievers: Review Kepler's First Law with these students and have reference materials available. Review the use of a protractor. These students can be paired with high achievers for this activity.

SCORING RUBRIC

Full credit can be given to students who conclude correctly that the two areas are the same, and that the planet moves faster when it is close to the Sun. Extra credit can be awarded to students who do the Extensions or any of the Follow-up Activities. The quiz can be scored from 1 to 4 correct.

 INTERNET TIE-INS   http://windows.ivv.nasa.gov/the_universe/uts/kepler2.html

 QUIZ
1. State Kepler's Second Law in one sentence.
2. Does a planet move faster in its orbit when it is near the Sun or when it is farther from the Sun?
3. During what month is the Earth closest to the Sun, and during what month is it farthest from the Sun?
4. When does the Earth travel fastest in its orbit and when does it travel slowest?

Name _____ Date _____

Figure 3

18

Kepler's Second Law: How Do Planets Move?

☼ BEFORE YOU BEGIN ☼

Johannes Kepler (1571–1630) discovered three rules that govern how planets orbit the Sun. These rules are called Kepler's Laws. The first of these laws describes the shape of a planetary orbit as an ellipse, with the Sun at one focus of the ellipse. In this activity you will examine Kepler's Second Law, which describes how a planet changes speed as it moves in its orbit.

Kepler's Second Law states that a line connecting the Sun and any planet sweeps out equal areas in a given length of time (say, one month). That is true regardless of where the planet is in its orbit or how far it is from the Sun at that time. As shown in Figure 1, the two shaded areas are equal. For this to be true, the planet must move faster when it is closer to the Sun, in order to cover a greater distance along its orbit, than when it is farther from the Sun. For example, the Earth is closest to the Sun in January, and farthest in July. So the Earth must move faster in its orbit in January than in July.

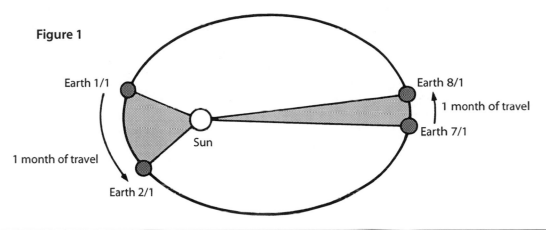

Figure 1

Earth 1/1

Earth 8/1

1 month of travel

Earth 7/1

Sun

1 month of travel

Earth 2/1

MATERIALS

- Pen or pencil
- Calculator
- Protractor
- Ruler
- Access to a photocopier

PROCEDURE

Share the tasks in steps 1–5 with your partner. Each of you should do steps 6–8 separately and enter your answers in the Data Collection and Analysis section.

Figure 2 shows an ellipse with the Sun's position at one focus. This ellipse is only for demonstration. Real planetary orbits in our solar system are much closer to circles. The major axis (the longest dimension) of the ellipse is drawn in for you. Remember that the Sun lies on the major axis. You will draw in two sectors, representing equal intervals of time during a planet's orbit around the Sun.

(continued)

Name _____   Date _____

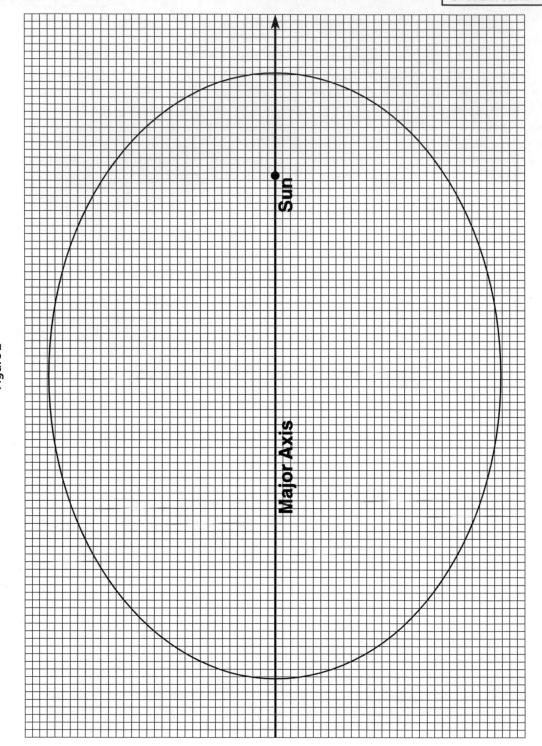

Figure 2

(continued)

Kepler's Second Law: How Do Planets Move? *(continued)*

1. Hold Figure 2 so that the arrow on the major axis points up. Line up the protractor with its center on the Sun and the 90° mark along the major axis, pointing in the direction of the arrow. Mark an angle that is 53° to either side of the 90° direction. That is, make marks at 37° and 143°.

2. Use the ruler to draw two straight lines extending from the Sun to the ellipse along each of the angle marks you just made. Label the area enclosed by these two lines and the arc segment of the ellipse as Sector A.

3. Now, turn the paper so that the arrow points down. Line up the protractor with its center on the Sun and the 90° mark along the major axis, pointing away from the arrow. Mark an angle that is 5° clockwise from the 90° mark.

4. Use the ruler to draw a straight line extending from the Sun to the ellipse along the angle mark you just made. Label the area enclosed by the line you just made, the major axis, and the arc segment of the ellipse, as Sector B.

5. With the sectors drawn and labeled, make two photocopies of Figure 2 so that each of you can do steps 6–8 independently.

6. Count the squares in each of the two sectors you just drew. It may be convenient to first count the complete squares, and then add the areas of the partial squares. For partial squares, estimate to the nearest $\frac{1}{4}$ square. Enter your values for the total area of each sector in the Data Collection and Analysis section.

7. Measure the length of the arc segment of the ellipse for each of the two sectors. Since these lines are curved, you cannot do this directly with the ruler. Try "rolling" the ruler along the curve from one end of the arc segment to the other. Another method is to break the arc segment into a number of small pieces (say, less than a centimeter long each) and then measure and add up the lengths of these pieces. You could also lay a piece of string along the arc and then measure the string. Record your results in the Data Collection and Analysis section.

8. Calculate the ratio of the length of the arc segment in Sector A to that of Sector B. Record your results in the Data Collection and Analysis section.

EXTENSION

Draw in a third sector, Sector C. With the arrow pointing to the right, line up the protractor with the center of the protractor on the Sun and the 0° mark along the major axis. Mark an angle at 90° (straight up). Mark another angle that is 30° counterclockwise from the 90° direction. Draw the lines to make a sector, and measure the area and arc segment length of the sector.

(continued)

Kepler's Second Law: How Do Planets Move? *(continued)*

📏 DATA COLLECTION AND ANALYSIS

Area of Sector A   _____ squares
Area of Sector B   _____ squares

Length of Sector A arc   _____ millimeters
Length of Sector B arc   _____ millimeters
Ratio of arc A to arc B   _____

EXTENSION
Area of Sector C   _____ squares
Length of Sector C arc   _____ millimeters

❓ CONCLUDING QUESTIONS

1. Are the areas of Sectors A and B equal or unequal? (Consider them equal if your measurements are the same to within 10% of each other, unequal otherwise.)

   _____

2. What is the ratio of the length of arc A to arc B? _____

   What do your results imply about the speed of a planet as it orbits the Sun? (Remember, Sectors A and B represent equal time intervals.) _____

   _____

3. If a planet had a perfectly circular orbit, how would its speed behave as it moved along in its orbit?

   _____

EXTENSION
Does Sector C represent the same time interval as Sectors A and B? Explain your answer.

☼ Follow-up Activities ☼

1. The planet whose positions led Kepler to conclude that orbits were ellipses was Mars. Figure 3 is an accurate representation of the shape of Mars' orbit. Obtain a copy of Figure 3 from your teacher. Do not add any labels or description. Show it to friends and family, and ask them to identify what geometric shape it is. Show as a bar graph how many people say it is a circle and how many say it is an ellipse (or oval). What do you think of Kepler's ability to determine the difference? Present your results to your class.

2. There are several interactive orbit simulators on the Internet, including http://www. explorescience.com/orbit.htm. There are also a number of freeware and shareware planetary motion simulators for Windows and Macintosh personal computers. Find and obtain access to one or more of these and spend some time examining the real orbits of planets, asteroids, and comets. Also make up your own orbits for hypothetical solar system objects. Some keywords to use in your search are *Kepler, orrery, planet, orbit,* and *simulator.*

Kepler's Third Law: Orbital Size and Period

 ## INSTRUCTIONAL OBJECTIVES

Students will be able to
- state Kepler's Third Law.
- describe how a planet's orbital size affects its period.

 ## NATIONAL SCIENCE STANDARDS ADDRESSED

Students demonstrate an understanding of
- predictable motion of the planets.

Students demonstrate scientific inquiry and problem-solving skills by
- identifying variables in experimental and non-experimental settings.

Students demonstrate effective scientific communication by
- representing data in multiple ways.
- arguing from evidence and data.

 ## MATERIALS

For each pair of students:
- Pen or pencil
- Calculator

HELPFUL HINTS AND DISCUSSION

Time frame: 40 minutes, or a single period
Structure: In pairs
Location: In class

It would be helpful for the students to do the activity on Kepler's First Law before they do this activity. That way, they would already be familiar with ellipses and understand what the semimajor axis is.

ADAPTATIONS FOR HIGH AND LOW ACHIEVERS

High Achievers: Encourage these students to do the Extension and Follow-up Activity. You can challenge these students to calculate planetary periods from semimajor axes and vice versa. They will have to know how to take roots as well as powers on their calculators.

Low Achievers: Review Kepler's First Law with these students and have reference materials available. Review how to take powers with a calculator. These students can be paired with high achievers for this activity.

SCORING RUBRIC

Full credit can be given to students who conclude correctly that the square of a planet's period (in years) is equal to the cube of its semimajor axis (in AU). Extra credit can be awarded to students who do the Extension or Follow-up Activity. The quiz can be scored from 1 to 4 correct.

 INTERNET TIE-INS   http://windows.ivv.nasa.gov/the_universe/uts/kepler3.html

QUIZ
1. State Kepler's Third Law in one sentence.
2. A planet farther from the Sun than Earth takes (*more* or *less*) time to complete one orbit around the Sun.
3. Define an astronomical unit.
4. Kepler's Laws are a special case of what more general physical law discovered later by Isaac Newton?

Kepler's Third Law: Orbital Size and Period

☼ BEFORE YOU BEGIN ☼

Kepler's three laws of planetary motion describe how the planets in our solar system orbit the Sun. The First Law says that the orbits of the planets are shaped like ellipses. The Second Law describes how a planet changes speed in its orbit, moving faster when it is closer to the Sun and more slowly when it is farther from the Sun. Kepler published his First and Second Laws in 1609. It took another 10 years of painstaking and repetitive calculation before he published the Third Law.

Kepler's Third Law describes the relationship between the size of a planet's orbit and the time it takes the planet to complete one orbit around the Sun. The size of an elliptical orbit is described by its semimajor axis, *a*. The Earth's orbital semimajor axis is defined to be 1 **astronomical unit**, abbreviated AU. The values of *a* for the other planets are expressed in AU, which gives the relative size of their orbits compared with Earth's orbit. The time it takes for a planet to complete one orbit is the **orbital period**, *P*. Earth's orbital period is defined to be 1 **year**. The values of *P* for the other planets are expressed in Earth years, which gives the time it takes for them to complete one orbit. Kepler's Third Law states that the square of the period, *P*, is equal to the cube of the semi-major axis, *a*. As an equation: $P^2 = a^3$

Isaac Newton, discoverer of the *Law of Universal Gravitation*, benefited from Kepler's earlier work. Newton realized that Kepler's Laws were a special case of gravity, namely, the case of a small mass (a planet) orbiting around a much larger mass (the Sun). Universal gravitation can be used not only to describe how planets orbit around the Sun, but how double stars orbit each other, and even how stars orbit around the center of our galaxy.

 **MATERIALS**

- Pen or pencil
- Calculator

 PROCEDURE

Table 1 in the Data Collection and Analysis section shows the orbital period (in Earth years) and semimajor axes (in astronomical units) for the nine planets.

1. For each planet, calculate the values for the square of the period and enter them in the spaces provided in Table 1. For the innermost four planets, round off to 3 decimal places in your answers. For the rest of the planets, do not include any decimal places in your answers.

2. For each planet, calculate the values for the cube of the semimajor axis and enter them in the spaces provided in Table 1. Round off your answers as in step 1.

(continued)

Name _____ Date _____

 DATA COLLECTION AND ANALYSIS

Table 1

Planet	P (years)	a (AU)	P^2	a^3
Mercury	0.24	0.387		
Venus	0.616	0.723		
Earth	1.000	1.000		
Mars	1.88	1.524		
Jupiter	11.9	5.2		
Saturn	29.5	9.54		
Uranus	84.0	19.2		
Neptune	165	30.2		
Pluto	249	39.5		

How do the values in the P^2 and a^3 columns of Table 1 compare? _____

_____

Is the agreement equally good for all planets? _____

CONCLUDING QUESTIONS

1. How does Kepler's Third Law predict that the values in the P^2 and a^3 columns of Table 1 should compare?

   _____

2. If a new planet were discovered beyond Pluto, how would its orbital period compare with Pluto's?

   _____

3. You are on an imaginary planet that orbits the Sun in the same plane as the other planets. If you orbit the Sun in 45 years, between which two planets must you be orbiting?

   _____

EXTENSION

For the imaginary planet in Concluding Question 3 above, calculate the semimajor axis in AU.

☀ Follow-up Activity ☀

Find the orbital period and semimajor axis for one of the minor planets (asteroids) orbiting between Mars and Jupiter. Calculate the square of the period and the cube of the semimajor axis. Do the minor planets obey Kepler's Third Law?

INSTRUCTIONAL OBJECTIVES

Students will be able to

- make a model of a forming solar system.
- describe how gravity affects the formation of objects in the solar system.

 NATIONAL SCIENCE STANDARDS ADDRESSED

Students demonstrate an understanding of

- the origin and evolution of the solar system.
- gravity.

Students demonstrate scientific inquiry and problem-solving skills by

- identifying and controlling variables in experimental research settings.

Students demonstrate effective scientific communication by

- arguing from evidence and data.

 MATERIALS

For each student:

- Access to a kitchen
- Large (at least 6-quart) soup pot or bowl
- Assorted spices, herbs, and grains
- Large spoon
- Watch or clock that can be read in seconds
- Cooking oil

EXTENSION

- Dishwashing liquid, or liquid laundry detergent

 INTERNET TIE-INS   http://www.anu.edu.au/Physics/nineplanets/origin.html
http://tqd.advanced.org/3461/proto.htm

QUIZ
1. What did the solar system form from, and how did the process begin?
2. How did the rotation of the solar nebula change as planets were forming?
3. What happened to smaller particles in the solar nebula that didn't form into planets?
4. What happened to material in orbit around planets, that couldn't form into moons?

HELPFUL HINTS AND DISCUSSION

Time frame: 40 minutes, or a single period
Structure: Individually
Location: At home

The success of this activity depends on the student's ability to carefully observe the distribution of material in the swirling water in the pot. The list of features in the Data Tables is meant to help guide this observation. It would be helpful if the students have seen one of the many animated movies or videos of the formation of the solar system prior to performing this activity.

ADAPTATIONS FOR HIGH AND LOW ACHIEVERS

High Achievers: Encourage these students to do the Extensions and Follow-up Activity.

Low Achievers: Encourage these students to do this activity with a parent or sibling. Review the concept that objects in space attract each other because of gravitational forces.

SCORING RUBRIC

Full credit can be given to students whose observations demonstrate that they followed the directions and recognized the features in the data tables, and who answer the Concluding Questions correctly and in complete sentences. Extra credit can be awarded to students who do the Extensions or Follow-up Activity. The quiz can be scored from 1 to 4 correct.

Name _____   Date _____

☼ BEFORE YOU BEGIN ☼

Astronomers believe that the solar system formed when a cloud of gas and dust in space began to shrink due to the force of its own gravity. This "solar nebula" was spinning very slowly. As it continued to shrink, the force of gravity became even stronger. It concentrated the gas and dust in the center, eventually forming the Sun. At the same time, the rest of the solar nebula rotated faster and faster, just as an ice skater speeds up when she brings her arms in while spinning. The rotating nebula flattened into a disk. The small objects in this disk were clumped together into larger ones by increasing gravitational attraction. Eventually some of these objects grew to be the size of the planets we know today. Many smaller objects were either blown out beyond Pluto or continue to float in interplanetary space. Figure 1, a–d, illustrates this idea (not to scale). In the asteroid belt, between the orbits of Mars and Jupiter, conditions were apparently not quite right to actually form a planet. So, we are left with a large number of small objects in separate orbits around the Sun.

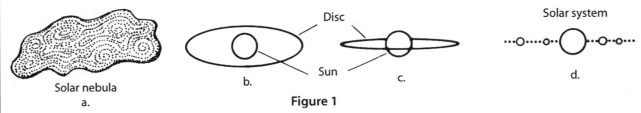

Solar nebula
a.

Disc

Sun
b.

c.

Solar system

d.

Figure 1

The same basic process occurred on a smaller scale during the formation of systems of moons around the giant planets, Jupiter, Saturn, Uranus, and Neptune. In each case, a disk formed around the planet, eventually giving rise to a family of moons. In locations where moons could not form, rings were left behind. The most spectacular of these belong to Saturn.

 ## MATERIALS

- Access to a kitchen
- Large (at least 6-quart) soup pot or bowl
- Assorted spices, herbs, and grains

- Large spoon
- Watch or clock that can be read in seconds
- Cooking oil

EXTENSION • Dishwashing liquid or liquid laundry detergent

 ## PROCEDURE

1. Fill the pot half-full with water at about room temperature. Let it sit for a few minutes to allow the water to stop moving.

2. Sprinkle small amounts of four to six assorted spices, herbs, and grains into the pot. Possible choices are rice (2 tbsp), cornmeal (1 tbsp), bran (1 tbsp), black pepper ($\frac{1}{2}$ tsp), dill ($\frac{1}{2}$ tsp), basil ($\frac{1}{2}$ tsp), oregano ($\frac{1}{2}$ tsp), and crushed red pepper ($\frac{1}{2}$ tsp). Feel free to try others.

3. Review the list of features you will be looking for in Data Table 1 (next page). You might see some or all of these features at various times as your "solar nebula" develops. You may ask family members or friends to help you make the observations called for in Step 4.

(continued)

Name _____   Date _____

4. Using the spoon, stir the water in the pot with a circular motion to get the water swirling in one direction. Quickly remove the spoon. Counting time from the moment you remove the spoon, observe the contents of the pot at the times listed, looking specifically for the features you reviewed in step 3. At each observation time, make a check mark in the appropriate box in Data Table 1 for each feature visible at that time. Some of the features are obvious; others may take some practice to identify. If you are not sure of your results, stir the pot again and repeat your observations.

5. You can change the conditions of your forming "solar system" by changing the local force of "gravity." Increase the simulated gravity between particles in your "solar nebula" by adding 1–2 tablespoons of cooking oil, and repeat step 4. Record your observations in Data Table 2.

DATA COLLECTION AND ANALYSIS

Data Table 1 (Step 4)

Feature	1 sec	15 sec	30 sec	2 min	5 min
All materials evenly mixed throughout water					
Floating material evenly spread over surface					
Pile of material in center at bottom of pot					
Smooth ring on surface					
Lumpy ring on surface					
Material touching pot on surface					
No material touching pot on surface					
Small clumps of particles on surface					
Large clumps on surface					
Single lumpy disk on surface					

Data Table 2 (Step 5)

Feature	1 sec	15 sec	30 sec	2 min	5 min
All materials evenly mixed throughout water					
Floating material evenly spread over surface					
Pile of material in center at bottom of pot					
Smooth ring on surface					
Lumpy ring on surface					
Material touching pot on surface					
No material touching pot on surface					
Small clumps of particles on surface					
Large clumps on surface					
Single lumpy disk on surface					

(continued)

Making a Solar System *(continued)*

EXTENSION

In step 5 you changed the conditions of the "solar nebula" by changing the simulated force of gravity. To decrease "gravity," add 2 tablespoons of dishwashing liquid or liquid laundry detergent, and repeat step 4. This time only make note of the features present at the end of 5 minutes. Your result should be quite different from your previous results.

CONCLUDING QUESTIONS

1. Why does the mass of material that sinks to the bottom of the pot represent the Sun?

   _____

2. How does gravity between particles in the disk affect what eventually forms from the disk?

   _____

   _____

3. What features in the real solar system do the features listed in Data Tables 1 and 2 correspond to (answer "none" for a feature with no parallel in the real solar system)? _____

   _____

   _____

4. If the force of gravity between particles in the disk had been greater when the solar system formed, would the planets likely be larger or smaller than they are now?

   _____

EXTENSION

What might the solar system be like if the force of gravity between particles in the disk had been much weaker than it actually was?

☀ Follow-up Activity ☀

Write a brief research report comparing the ring systems around the gas giant planets, Jupiter, Saturn, Uranus, and Neptune. Include the year the rings were first observed, how they were discovered, the composition of the rings, and the relationship of the diameters of the rings to the orbits of the planets' moons. Explain the formation of rings in more detail than presented in the Before You Begin section of this activity.

Composition of the Planets

 INSTRUCTIONAL OBJECTIVES

Students will be able to

- describe the varying composition of the planets.
- understand the cause of the varying composition of the planets.

 NATIONAL SCIENCE STANDARDS ADDRESSED

Students demonstrate an understanding of

- evolution of the solar system.
- effects of heat and pressure.

Students demonstrate scientific inquiry and problem-solving skills by

- identifying variables in a nonexperimental setting.
- using relevant concepts to explain phenomena.
- working in teams to collect and share information and ideas.

Students demonstrate effective scientific communication by

- arguing from evidence and data.
- representing data in multiple ways.

 MATERIALS

For each group of two or three students:

- 1000-ml graduated cylinder
- Triple-beam balance
- Ice cube
- An ordinary stone, about the size of a Ping-Pong ball
- Steel nuts, bolts, or washers (totaling about 250 g)
- 8.5" × 11" sheet of paper
- Pen or pencil
- Ruler

HELPFUL HINTS AND DISCUSSION

Time frame: 40 minutes, or a single period
Structure: In groups of two or three students
Location: In class

A 1000-ml graduated cylinder is needed so that the students can measure changes in water level to the nearest ml or so. The mouth must be wide enough for the ice cube, the stone, and the steel parts to fit. Students should exercise great care when dropping the stone and the steel parts into the graduated cylinder so that it doesn't crack.

For Part A, step 7, each team will need about 250 g of steel. You can preassemble piles of steel nuts, bolts, and/or washers to make up this mass. Be sure you don't have parts made of brass, aluminum, or other metals. You can check this with a magnet. You may supply a collection of stones for the students to pick from, or ask them to collect appropriate stones before doing the activity.

Have a supply of ice cubes available. Remind the students to measure the mass of the ice cube as quickly as possible and to get it into the graduated cylinder of water. They will have to submerge the ice cube to measure its volume. The tip of a pencil or a paper clip may be used to just barely keep the ice cube submerged while a partner reads the volume in the beaker.

ADAPTATIONS FOR HIGH AND LOW ACHIEVERS

High Achievers: Encourage these students to do the Extension and Follow-up Activities.

Low Achievers: Have a reference book available for these students. Review the concept of density, and the idea that density can be calculated if you know mass and volume. Also review the operation of the triple-beam balance and how to read the volume of liquid in a beaker or graduated cylinder. You can group low achievers with high achievers for this exercise.

SCORING RUBRIC

Full credit can be given to students whose measurements and calculations of density are approximately correct (ice = 0.92 g/cm^3, stone = 2.7 g/cm^3, steel = 7.7 g/cm^3). Extra credit can be given to students who do the Extension or a Follow-up Activity. The quiz can be scored from 1 to 4 correct.

  INTERNET TIE-INS   http://www.hawastsoc.org/solar/eng/solarsys.htm#comp

QUIZ   1. Name the terrestrial planets and describe their composition.
2. Name the gas giant planets and describe their composition.
3. In the early solar system, how did temperature in the gas disk change with distance from the Sun?
4. In the early solar system, why could ice condense only far from the Sun?

Name _____   Date _____

Composition of the Planets

☼ BEFORE YOU BEGIN ☼

As you read this you are sitting on top of the solid rocky crust of our planet. Deep inside Earth is a denser core made of iron, nickel, and sulfur. On Mercury, Mars, or Venus, you would also be sitting on rocky crust above a denser metallic core. These four innermost planets are called the **terrestrial planets** because they are similar to Earth (*Terra* in Latin) in structure and composition. But you could not be sitting at all on Jupiter, Saturn, Uranus, or Neptune, because these planets have no solid surface. These are called the **gas giant planets**, because they are huge compared to Earth and are composed mostly of light gases like hydrogen and methane, with only a small rocky core deep in their centers. The enormous difference in composition and structure between terrestrial planets and gas giant planets tells us a great deal about conditions affecting planet formation in the early solar system. We do not consider Pluto here because its history is thought to be quite different from that of the rest of the planets.

The birth of the planets began as the Sun was forming at the center of the young solar system. A wide disk of leftover gas that formed the basis of the planets orbited around the young Sun. This wide disk of gas contained light compounds (hydrogen, water, methane, ammonia . . .), plus the elements that make up rock and metal. This disk was hotter closer in toward the Sun and cooler farther away. As the entire disk cooled with time, some of the gas was able to condense, depending on the distance from the Sun. Closer in, rock and metal could condense, but water and other light gases could not. Farther out, even the light compounds could condense into solid form, known as ices. The inner (terrestrial) planets are therefore small and made up primarily of rock and metal. Because more material could condense farther from the Sun, the outer planets (gas giants) grew large and contain a great deal of ice and gas in addition to the rock and metal at their cores. Because of their great mass, the gravity of the giant planets compresses the gas until it has a density comparable to water.

 ## MATERIALS

- 1000-ml graduated cylinder
- Triple-beam balance
- Ice cube
- An ordinary stone, about the size of a Ping-Pong ball

- Steel nuts, bolts, or washers (totaling about 250 g)
- 8.5" × 11" sheet of paper
- Pen or pencil
- Ruler

 ## PROCEDURE

Part A

1. Fill the graduated cylinder with about 800 ml of water. Read the exact volume and record this value in Part A, Section 1, of the Data Collection and Analysis section. Remember that you must read the water level at the bottom of the meniscus, and that 1 ml is equal to 1 cm^3.

(continued)

Composition of the Planets *(continued)*

2. Measure the mass of an ice cube in grams with the triple-beam balance. Work as quickly as possible to minimize the amount of water lost from the ice cube. Record your value in Part A, Section 1, of the Data Collection and Analysis section.

3. As soon as you have measured the ice cube's mass, place it into the graduated cylinder. Using a paper clip or the tip of a pencil, push down on the ice cube so that it is just barely submerged. One of you should read the volume of water and ice in the cylinder from the new water level and record it in Part A, Section 1, of the Data Collection and Analysis section.

4. Subtract the original water volume from the level you measured in step 3 and enter the result as the "change in volume" in Part A, Section 1, of the Data Collection and Analysis section. The "change in volume" represents the volume of the ice cube.

5. Calculate the density of the ice cube. Density equals mass divided by volume. You have already measured the mass of the ice cube, and its volume is the "change in volume" you calculated in step 4. Enter your result, in g/cm^3, in Part A, Section 1, of the Data Collection and Analysis section.

6. Repeat steps 1–5 using the stone instead of the ice cube. Record your results in Part A, Section 2, of the Data Collection and Analysis section.

7. Repeat steps 1–5 using the steel parts instead of the ice cube. Record your results in Part A, Section 3, of the Data Collection and Analysis section.

Part B

1. Hold Figure 1 horizontally (as it appears on the page). Using the data in Data Table 1, make a vertical mark 1 cm high with a pen or pencil at the density value of each planet listed. The mark for Earth has been made for you. Above each mark write the name of the corresponding planet.

2. Now make marks 2 cm high for ice, stone, and steel, using your results from Part A. Label them "Ice," "Rock," and "Iron," respectively (steel is mostly iron).

Data Table 1

Planet	Density (g/cm^3)
Mercury	5.43
Venus	5.24
Earth	5.52
Mars	3.93
Jupiter	1.33
Saturn	0.69
Uranus	1.32
Neptune	1.64

(continued)

Name _____   Date _____

Composition of the Planets *(continued)*

 DATA COLLECTION AND ANALYSIS

Part A

Section 1

Mass of ice cube: _____ g

Volume of water alone: _____ cm^3

Volume of water + ice: _____ cm^3

Change in volume: _____ cm^3

Density of ice cube = mass of ice cube/change in volume = _____ g/cm^3

Section 2

Mass of stone: _____ g

Volume of water alone: _____ cm^3

Volume of water + stone: _____ cm^3

Change in volume: _____ cm^3

Density of stone = mass of stone/change in volume = _____ g/cm^3

Section 3

Mass of steel: _____ g

Volume of water alone: _____ cm^3

Volume of water + steel: _____ cm^3

Change in volume: _____ cm^3

Density of steel = mass of steel/change in volume = _____ g/cm^3

Part B

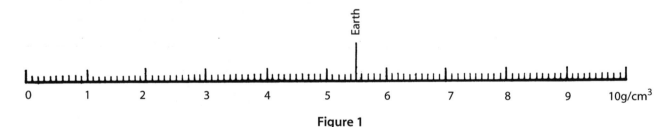

Figure 1

(continued)

Composition of the Planets *(continued)*

❓ CONCLUDING QUESTIONS

1. List the three materials you measured in order of increasing density.

   _____

   _____

   _____

2. Given a sample of unknown material, describe one way you might determine if it is more similar to ice, rock, or iron.

   _____

   _____

3. Looking at Figure 1, determine the two main types of material (of ice, rock, or iron) in each of the planets in Data Table 1. For this activity, we can consider ice and compressed gases to be similar materials.

   _____

EXTENSION

Look up the density of the Earth's moon. Add it to Figure 1, and see what the moon might be made of. Look up the densities of the moons of Jupiter and Saturn. Add these objects to Figure 1, and try to figure out what these objects might be made of.

☼ Follow-up Activities ☼

1. Using the procedure described in Part A, measure the density of a variety of other materials. Can materials be identified reliably based solely on their densities?

2. Investigate the composition of the planets in greater detail, using astronomy texts, the Web, and other resources. Based on your findings, speculate on what objects in the solar system, besides Earth, might support life. Note that liquid water has a density similar to but slightly higher than ice.

Albedo

 INSTRUCTIONAL OBJECTIVES

Students will be able to

- define the albedo of a solar system object.
- describe the albedo of various solar system objects.

 NATIONAL SCIENCE STANDARDS ADDRESSED

Students demonstrate an understanding of

- interactions of energy and matter; absorption and emission of light.

Students demonstrate scientific inquiry and problem-solving skills by

- identifying variables in experimental and non-experimental settings.

Students demonstrate effective scientific communication by

- arguing from evidence and data.

 MATERIALS

For each student:

- A rock
- Snow (or frost in a household freezer)
- A piece of charcoal
- A concrete sidewalk
- The plastic case of a personal computer
- A piece of white paper
- A painted wall
- An automobile tire
- The bark of a tree
- A lampshade
  EXTENSION
- An inexpensive pair of cardboard "3-D" glasses

HELPFUL HINTS AND DISCUSSION

Time frame: 40 minutes over the course of several days
Structure: Individually
Location: At home and at other locations

When you photocopy the Data Table with its gray scale for the class, be careful to set the photocopier's darkness or contrast so that all 21 of the gray level steps (from full white to full black) are clearly visible on the copies. We suggest that you give the students several days to find and evaluate the objects and substances mentioned in Step 2. Note that, except for the Extension, the Materials section does not contain items that you need to supply to the students—these are items they will need to find on their own to do the exercise. The "3-D" glasses specified for the Extension are the kind with red plastic and blue plastic for the lenses.

ADAPTATIONS FOR HIGH AND LOW ACHIEVERS

High Achievers: Encourage these students to do the Extension and Follow-up Activity.

Low Achievers: Have reference materials available for these students.

SCORING RUBRIC

Full credit can be given to students who get approximately correct albedos for the common objects listed (snow or frost is about 1, charcoal is about 0, etc.); who properly place the solar system objects on the albedo scale; and who answer the Concluding Questions correctly and in complete sentences. Extra credit can be awarded to students who do the Extension or Follow-up Activity. The quiz can be scored from 1 to 4 correct.

 INTERNET TIE-INS   http://zebu.uoregon.edu/~js/glossary/albedo.html

 QUIZ   1. Define albedo.
2. How can the moon look so bright when it has such a low albedo?
3. Why does Venus have a high albedo?
4. Why does the Earth's albedo vary?

Name _____ Date _____

Albedo

☀ **BEFORE YOU BEGIN** ☀

Recall a time when you looked up at the full moon on a cloudless night. The moon seems so bright and white, you might imagine it to be covered in something highly reflective like snow or talcum powder. But looks are deceiving. In fact, if you held a piece of the moon's surface in your hand it would appear very dark indeed. The moon only appears bright in the sky because it is illuminated by a tremendous amount of light from the Sun. The fraction of the light falling on a solar system object that is then reflected back into space is called its **albedo**. The albedo of an object can range from nearly zero (no light reflected back) to almost 1 (all light reflected back).

Observing the albedo of an object can help to determine what it is made of. A low albedo probably indicates a surface composed of basalts and other dark rocks, as on the moon. A high albedo is often due to the presence of clouds, as on Venus, or of a frozen, icy surface, as on some of the moons of the gas giant planets. Earth's albedo is less predictable. It varies widely because of the presence of oceans and because of large variations in cloud cover.

Albedo is also important in understanding the surface conditions on a solar system object. For objects with little or no atmosphere, a low albedo means that much of the incoming light from the Sun is absorbed. The object will be relatively warm for its distance from the Sun. Similar objects with a high albedo absorb less Sunlight and so are colder. For objects with atmospheres, the situation is more complicated. Venus has a high albedo because of its perpetual thick cloud layer, but its surface temperature is very high because any light energy that does penetrate the clouds gets trapped below them, a condition called the **greenhouse effect**. The wide variation in the Earth's albedo is an important factor in studies of long-term climate and global warming.

 MATERIALS

- A rock
- Snow (or frost in a household freezer)
- A piece of charcoal
- A concrete sidewalk
- The plastic case of a personal computer

- A piece of white paper
- A painted wall
- An automobile tire
- The bark of a tree
- A lampshade

For the Extension:
- An inexpensive pair of cardboard "3D" glasses

 PROCEDURE

You will use the gray scale (column of gray rectangles) in the Data Collection and Analysis section to estimate the albedos of some common objects or substances. You may find these objects at home, at school, or outdoors. These can then be compared with the albedos of selected solar system objects.

1. Fold the sheet of paper with the gray scale so that the left edge of the gray scale is at the left edge of the paper.

(continued)

Albedo *(continued)*

2. For each of the objects in the Materials list, hold the left edge of the gray scale up against the object and estimate which gray scale rectangle is closest to the same brightness (or darkness) as the object. Then write the name of the object to the right of the best-matching rectangle in the column labeled "Ordinary Objects" in the Data Collection and Analysis section. The number in that row, in the column labeled "Albedo," is the albedo value of that rectangle. Try to measure as many of the listed objects as you can. If you cannot find all of the objects listed, pick some other common objects and add them to your table. Try to avoid choosing brightly colored objects, which are hard to compare with the gray rectangles. It's OK to have more than one object in a single box in the Data Collection and Analysis table.

3. In the "Solar System Objects" column of the data table, write the name of each solar system object from Table 1 in the row that best corresponds to its albedo. Again, it's OK to have more than one object in a single box in the data table.

Table 1

Object	Type of Object	Albedo
Mercury	planet	0.06
Venus	planet	0.76
Earth	planet	0.4 (average)
Moon	moon of Earth	0.07
Mars	planet	0.16
Phobos	moon of Mars	0.018
Ceres	asteroid	0.01
Vesta	asteroid	0.38
Jupiter	planet	0.51
Europa	moon of Jupiter	0.6
Callisto	moon of Jupiter	0.2
Saturn	planet	0.50
Titan	moon of Saturn	0.20
Uranus	planet	0.66
Oberon	moon of Uranus	0.05
Neptune	planet	0.62
Triton	moon of Neptune	0.80
Pluto	planet	0.5
Charon	moon of Pluto	0.38

(continued)

Name _____   Date _____

 DATA COLLECTION AND ANALYSIS

Albedo	Ordinary Objects	Solar System Objects
0.00		
0.05		
0.10		
0.15		
0.20		
0.25		
0.30		
0.35		
0.40		
0.45		
0.50		
0.55		
0.60		
0.65		
0.70		
0.75		
0.80		
0.85		
0.90		
0.95		
1.00		

(continued)

Name _____ Date _____

Albedo *(continued)*

❓ CONCLUDING QUESTIONS

1. Which solar system body in Table 1 has the highest albedo? _____

   The lowest? _____

2. Which of the objects you measured has the highest albedo? _____

   The lowest? _____

3. Is the albedo of the moon more like that of a snowball or a lump of charcoal?

   _____

4. Based on albedo, what can you speculate about the composition of the surface of Triton?
   Mars? Ceres?

   _____

   _____

   _____

5. Why don't we ever speak about the albedo of the Sun?

   _____

   _____

EXTENSION

Many objects on Earth and in space have a distinctly colored appearance. In astronomy, a solar system object may have different albedos in different colors of light. This fact can be an additional clue to the object's surface composition. "3-D" glasses have a red filter and a blue filter as lenses. Pick a brightly colored object, like an orange. Looking through the **red** side of the 3-D glasses, compare the object with the gray scale and determine its albedo in red light. You may have to provide strong illumination to the area to see both the object and the gray scale well. Repeat the process, this time looking through the blue side of the 3-D glasses. Compare the "red" and "blue" albedos you found—are they approximately equal?

☼ Follow-up Activity ☼

The albedo of Earth is such a critical factor in understanding climate and global warming that it has become a very important quantity to measure. From the Internet and other sources find out all you can about Earth's albedo, including its variation around the surface of the planet, how it changes with the seasons, how it is measured, and what the effects of global warming might be on Earth's average albedo. Write a brief report on what you learned.

INSTRUCTIONAL OBJECTIVES

Students will be able to

- describe advances in our knowledge of solar system objects.
- appreciate the impact of technology on our understanding of the solar system.

 NATIONAL SCIENCE STANDARDS ADDRESSED

Students demonstrate an understanding of

- evolution of the solar system.

Students demonstrate scientific inquiry and problem-solving skills by

- using evidence from reliable sources.

Students demonstrate effective scientific communication by

- arguing from evidence and data.

 MATERIALS

For each student:

Internet access, especially to the following suggested sites:

- http://spaceart.com/solar/eng/homepage.htm
- http://seds.lpl.arizona.edu/nineplanets/nineplanets/nineplanets.html
- http://observe.ivv.nasa.gov/nasa/gallery/image_gallery/solar_system/solar.html
- http://www.reston.com/astro/bio.web.html
- http://www.jpl.nasa.gov/solarsystem/
- http://www.syz.com/images/

 INTERNET TIE-INS   See the Materials section.

 QUIZ   1. Which new capabilities have allowed us to learn a great deal more about the solar system?
2. How did spacecraft change our understanding of the Cassini Division in Saturn's rings?
3. What did spacecraft discover happening on Neptune's moon, Triton?

HELPFUL HINTS AND DISCUSSION

Time frame: 40 minutes, possibly over several days
Structure: Individually
Location: In class or at home

This activity is something of a solar system "scavenger hunt." The students will find data on the World Wide Web, using the included URL's as a starting point. They only need to find a subset of the objects that are listed in the exercise. Three are suggested, but you can vary the number required.

ADAPTATIONS FOR HIGH AND LOW ACHIEVERS

High Achievers: Encourage these students to do the Extension and Follow-up Activities.

Low Achievers: Have reference materials available for these students.

SCORING RUBRIC

Full credit can be given to students who find the requested data for the required number of objects, and who answer the Concluding Questions correctly and in complete sentences. Extra credit can be awarded to students who find the requested data for additional objects, or who do the Extension or Follow-up Activities. The quiz can be scored from 1 to 3 correct.

Picture Gallery

☼ **BEFORE YOU BEGIN** ☼

Even before the beginning of space travel, people were fascinated by pictures of astronomical objects, including the planets. The red color and mysterious markings on Mars, the beautiful rings of Saturn, and the Great Red Spot on Jupiter have each been the subject of many thousands of photographs taken over the years through Earth-based telescopes.

Over the past generation, the ability to send spacecraft to distant parts of the solar system and to place large telescopes in orbit around Earth has led to an explosion in our knowledge of the solar system. Much of this knowledge has come from taking better pictures using electronic cameras and by simply getting closer to the objects. Old myths have been shattered. Mars is not covered with canals, as once thought. A dark band in Saturn's rings, called the **Cassini Division**, was thought to be empty, but was revealed to contain small particles that do not reflect light back toward us very well. Many new surprises have been uncovered. For example, Neptune's moon, Triton, was found to have geysers spewing nitrogen into its atmosphere. Above all, the solar system has been revealed as a place of extraordinary beauty.

In this activity, you will search the World Wide Web for images of solar system objects, and discover what has been learned from space-based observatories and interplanetary probes.

 MATERIALS

Internet access, especially to the following suggested sites:

- http://spaceart.com/solar/eng/homepage.htm
- http://seds.lpl.arizona.edu/nineplanets/nineplanets/nineplanets.html
- http://observe.ivv.nasa.gov/nasa/gallery/image_gallery/solar_system/solar.html
- http://www.reston.com/astro/bio.web.html
- http://www.jpl.nasa.gov/solarsystem/
- http://www.syz.com/images/

 PROCEDURE

1. For any three of the solar system objects in Table 1, search the World Wide Web to find an image taken from space (either from a telescope orbiting Earth or from an interplanetary spacecraft) that shows at least one of the listed features.

2. For each object, enter the following in Data Table 1 in the Data Collection and Analysis section:

    • the complete URL (Web address) at which you found the image;

    • the telescope or mission which obtained the image;

    • at least one important fact about the object that was not known from Earth-based observations;

    • a detailed description of the image.

    If you have a printer available, print out a copy of the image.

3. While searching for the objects listed, you will come across many other images. Make notes in the Data Collection and Analysis section about anything you find interesting.

(continued)

Name _____   Date _____

Table 1

Object	Features to Be Found in Image
Venus	• Volcano (seen on radar images) • Rocks on the surface
Mars	• Olympus Mons • Valles Marineris • Red sand and rocks on the surface
Phobos (moon of Mars)	• Stickney crater
Ida (asteroid)	• Dactyl (Ida's natural satellite)
Jupiter	• Dark patches made by impacts of Comet Shoemaker-Levy 9
Io (moon of Jupiter)	• Sulfur volcano caught while erupting!
Callisto (moon of Jupiter)	• Chain of impact craters in a straight line • Valhalla (giant impact crater)
Saturn	• "Spokes" in its rings • Braided rings
Enceladus (moon of Saturn)	• Smooth plains
Comet Halley	• Dark nucleus, with gas and dust erupting from it
Neptune	• Bright clouds • Rings

(continued)

Name _____ Date _____

 DATA COLLECTION AND ANALYSIS

Data Table 1

Object	URL
	Telescope or Mission
	Important Fact (not known from Earth observation)
	Description of the Image

NOTES:

(continued)

Picture Gallery *(continued)*

CONCLUDING QUESTIONS

1. What kinds of features do we see on solar system objects though space-based observation that we do not see from Earth?

   _____

   _____

   _____

2. From the images you saw, what are some of the common features of planets and moons with solid surfaces?

   _____

   _____

   _____

3. From the images you saw, what are some of the common features of the "gas giant" planets (Jupiter, Saturn, Uranus, Neptune)?

   _____

   _____

   _____

EXTENSION

Some solar system objects have now been observed from Earth-based telescopes, by interplanetary spacecraft missions, and by the Hubble Space Telescope. Find representative images of all three types of observation, and compare their quality. What can you see in one that you can't see in another? Most planetary missions only visit a planet or other object briefly as they fly past, although some go into orbit around the object and operate for months. What kinds of observation are still done best by Earth-based instruments?

☼ Follow-up Activities ☼

1. Every planet except Pluto has been visited by a spacecraft from Earth, some more than once. Research these missions and make a poster showing the planets labeled with the names and arrival dates of the spacecraft that have visited them.

2. Find out the names of all current interplanetary spacecraft missions. Include those that are at their destination and still working, as well as those that are on the way to their target planet(s).

The Phases of the Moon

 INSTRUCTIONAL OBJECTIVES

Students will be able to

- describe the changes in the appearance of the moon as the cycle of phases progresses.
- explain why phases of the moon occur.

NATIONAL SCIENCE STANDARDS ADDRESSED

Students demonstrate an understanding of

- moon phases.

Students demonstrate scientific inquiry and problem-solving skills by

- using concepts to explain a variety of observations and phenomena.

Students demonstrate effective scientific communication by

- arguing from evidence and data.
-
- representing data in multiple ways.

 MATERIALS

For each pair of students:

- Floor lamp with bare bulb (60–100 watts at home, 150 watts in class)
- Box, stepstool, or chair
- Room that can be darkened
- Extension cord
- Masking tape
- White Ping-Pong ball to represent the moon
- Dowel or stick (such as handle end of wooden spoon), about 1 foot long
- Adhesive putty
- 8.5" × 11" piece of drawing paper

 INTERNET TIE-INS

http://tycho.usno.navy.mil:80/srss.html
http://fourmilab.ch/earthview/uplanet.html

HELPFUL HINTS AND DISCUSSION

Time frame: 40 minutes, or a single period
Structure: In pairs
Location: In class or at home

If you are doing the activity in class, students can share a single darkened room and light source. The light source will have to be very strong, at least a 150-watt incandescent lamp. Caution the students that the lamp will be very hot, and they are not to approach or touch it. If you place the lamp in the center of the room many students can use it at once. They should work at a distance of about 6 to 10 feet from the lamp. If students do the activity at home they can use a 60- to 100-watt incandescent lamp, at a distance of 3 to 6 feet. Instruct students to have the lamp and the Ping-Pong ball slightly above their heads in order to avoid casting shadows of themselves on the "moon."

ADAPTATIONS FOR HIGH AND LOW ACHIEVERS

High Achievers: Encourage high achievers to do the Extensions and Follow-up Activities.

Low Achievers: Have reference books available for these students. Review with them the fact that the moon shines by reflected sunlight, and that it is the part of the lit portion of the moon that we can see that determines the moon's phase.

SCORING RUBRIC

Full credit can be given to students who fill in the table reasonably and who answer the Concluding Questions adequately and in complete sentences. Extra credit can be given to students who do any Extension or Follow-up Activities. The quiz can be scored from 1 to 4 correct.

 QUIZ

1. Put the following phases of the moon between new moon and full moon in the correct order: first quarter, waxing crescent, waxing gibbous.
2. In which phase do you see more of the lit surface of the moon: gibbous or crescent?
3. How much of the moon's surface is lit by the Sun at any one time?
4. At the new moon, how much of the moon's lit side do you see?

Name _____   Date _____

The Phases of the Moon

☼ BEFORE YOU BEGIN ☼

Many objects in the night sky do not appear to change much, even over a person's entire life-time. But one object—the moon—changes its appearance noticeably from night to night. The moon is really a sphere, but we see it in the sky as a circle. The appearance of the moon goes from a whole lit circle (the **full moon**) to something less than a whole lit circle (the **gibbous moon**), to a half-circle (the **quarter moon**), to a **crescent moon**, to almost invisible (the **new moon**), and back again to the full moon. This cycle is called the **lunar month**. The different ways the moon appears are called **phases**.

Phases of the moon (**lunar phases**) come about because the moon orbits around the Earth. We see these phases because, like the planets, the moon does not generate its own light. It reflects some of the Sunlight that shines on it. Depending on the moon's position in its orbit, we see different amounts of the moon's lit side. Figure 1 shows the moon in orbit around the Earth. Notice that most phases, except the full moon, are visible during part of the day (on the bright side of the Earth) as well as part of the night. Figure 2 shows the phases as seen from Earth. In this activity you will simulate the moon's orbit around Earth to see how lunar phases are produced.

Figure 1: Phases of the Moon As It Orbits Earth, Looking Down on Earth's North Pole

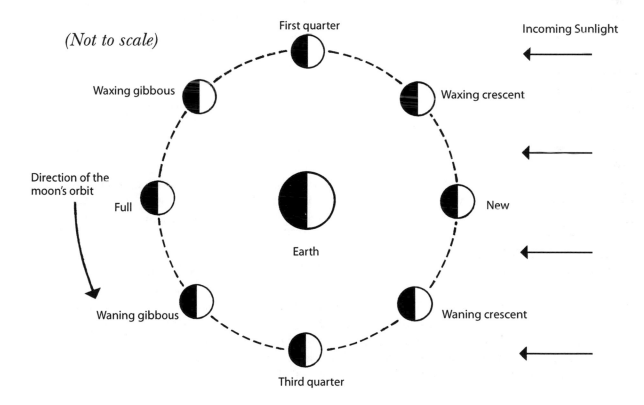

(continued)

Name _____ Date _____

Figure 2: What the Phases Look Like from Earth

New   Waxing crescent   First quarter   Waxing gibbous

Full   Waning gibbous   Third quarter   Waning crescent

 **MATERIALS**

- Floor lamp with bare bulb (60–100 watts at home, 150 watts in class)
- Box, stepstool, or chair
- Room that can be darkened
- Extension cord
- Masking tape

- White Ping-Pong ball to represent the moon
- Dowel or stick (such as handle end of wooden spoon), about 1 foot long
- 8.5" × 11" piece of drawing paper
- Adhesive putty

 PROCEDURE

1. Close all window shades and turn off all sources of light in the room except for one electric room light. You may need to turn that light off to check for additional sources of light, and then turn it back on so you can work safely. If you are doing the activity at home, try doing it after Sunset.
2. Place the lamp serving as the Sun near the center of the room if the activity is being done in class, and anywhere convenient if at home. Use a box to raise the bulb about a foot over your head. Plug it in, and, to avoid tripping, use the masking tape to cover any electrical extension cords you use.
3. Attach the Ping-Pong ball to one end of the dowel using the adhesive putty, as shown in Figure 3.
4. Turn on the Sun (the lamp on the box) and turn off the room lights. Stand about 1 to 3 meters from the Sun. Facing the Sun, hold up the dowel in front of you so that the Ping-Pong ball (the moon) is about at eye level. Hold the moon as steady as you can.
5. Have your partner examine the moon carefully from all angles, making sure not to get between the Sun and the moon (and cause an "eclipse"). Your partner should note what fraction ($\frac{1}{4}$, $\frac{2}{3}$, $\frac{1}{2}$, etc.) of the ***total*** surface of the Ping-Pong ball is lit. Turn the room lights back on, and have your partner record this fraction in his or her Data Collection and Analysis section. Look at Figure 1 to prove to yourself that this same fraction of the moon's surface is *always* lit.

(continued)

The Phases of the Moon (continued)

6. Switch places with your partner and repeat step 5.

   In steps 7–15, you and your partner should each do part and share results. That is, if you do steps 7, 8, 9, 10, and 11, your partner should do steps 12, 13, 14, and 15. You and your partner should make sketches for the steps you each did, so that between you, you have a full set of nine sketches.

7. Turn the room lights off again. Face the Sun, then turn 90° to the left so that the Sun appears to your right. Hold the dowel vertically out in front of you so that the Ping-Pong ball is just above the top of your head, as in Figure 4. Estimate the percentage of the half of the moon facing you that is lit, and enter this number in Table 1 in the Data Collection and Analysis section. Sketch the appearance of the moon on the drawing paper. Make sure to leave room for the eight additional sketches called for in steps 8–15. Label each sketch with the total angle through which you have turned.

8. Keeping the moon out in front of you and just above the top of your head, turn your body about 45° to the left and repeat step 7.

9. Turn another 45° to the left (90° total) and repeat step 7.

10. Turn another 45° to the left (135° total) and repeat step 7.

11. Turn another 45° to the left (180° total) and repeat step 7.

12. Turn another 45° to the left (225° total) and repeat step 7.

13. Turn another 45° to the left (270° total) and repeat step 7.

14. Turn another 45° to the left (315° total) and repeat step 7.

15. Turn another 45° to the left (360° total) and repeat step 7.

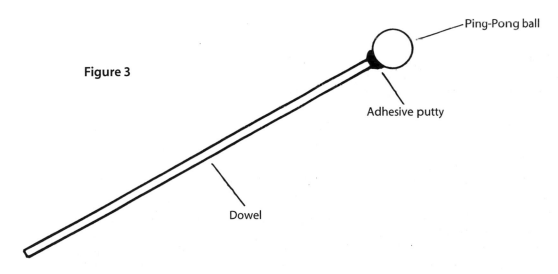

Figure 3

Ping-Pong ball

Adhesive putty

Dowel

(continued)

The Phases of the Moon *(continued)*

Figure 4

Light

EXTENSION

Some of the planets also undergo changes of phase similar to the moon's. First, by looking at a chart of the orbits of the planets, figure out which ones must always appear to us to be nearly fully lit by the Sun, and therefore do not exhibit phases. Now consider the remaining planets. By doing an exercise similar to the one described in this activity, determine and draw the phases they undergo as seen from Earth. For these planets, which phases are very difficult or impossible to actually observe? (Hint: the orbits of these planets are all in very nearly the same plane as the Earth's orbit around the Sun.)

 DATA COLLECTION AND ANALYSIS

In step 4, what fraction of the moon is lit?

Table 1

Position (°)	Percentage of the Half of the Moon Facing You That Is Lit	
Starting position (90° from facing the Sun)		Use drawing paper to sketch the phases of the moon.
+45°		
+90°		
+135°		
+180°		
+225°		
+270°		
+315°		
+360°		

(continued)

The Phases of the Moon (continued)

❔ CONCLUDING QUESTIONS

1. At any given time, how much of the moon's entire surface is lit by the Sun? _____

2. List the phases of the moon in chronological order, beginning with new moon.

   _____

   _____

   _____

   _____

3. What causes the phases of the moon?

   _____

   _____

EXTENSION

The Sun and the moon appear almost exactly the same size in the sky. If the moon's orbit around the Earth were exactly in the same plane as the Earth's orbit around the Sun, then during every new moon, the moon would cover the Sun to make a solar eclipse. During every full moon, the Earth would cover the Sun to make a lunar eclipse. Since solar and lunar eclipses occur rarely, what must be true about the moon's orbit relative to the Earth's orbit?

☼ Follow-up Activities ☼

1. Sometimes, when the moon is only a day or two past new, and is shining as a thin crescent, you can see the unlit part of the moon's side that faces us. This phenomenon is called **Earthshine**. Light from the Sun reflects off Earth, to the moon, and then back again to our eyes so we see faintly the entire circle of the moon. Look up the date of the next new moon in a newspaper or calendar or on the World Wide Web, and a day or two later, try to observe Earthshine.

2. Our civil calendar is based on the Sun. Calendars can also be based on the moon. For example, both the Jewish and Muslim calendars are based on the lunar cycle. Write a brief research report on one of these calendars.

3. Take a poll of students at your school. Ask them if the moon can ever be seen in the daytime. Make a bar graph showing the numbers of correct and incorrect answers.

4. Look up the origin of the English word *month*.

How Does the Moon Rotate?

 INSTRUCTIONAL OBJECTIVES

Students will be able to

- understand the moon's rotation as it relates to the moon's orbit.
- demonstrate synchronous rotation.

 NATIONAL SCIENCE STANDARDS ADDRESSED

Students demonstrate an understanding of

- origin and evolution of the Earth system.
- the predictable motion of the moon.

Students demonstrate scientific inquiry and problem-solving skills by

- identifying and controlling variables in experimental settings.
- working in teams to collect and share information and ideas.

Students demonstrate effective scientific communication by

- arguing from evidence and data.

 MATERIALS

For each pair of students:

- Styrofoam™ ball, about 3–5 inches in diameter
- Pushpin
- Wooden dowel, about ½ inch in diameter, about 1 foot long
- Marker
- Swivel chair

 INTERNET TIE-INS

http://seds.lpl.arizona.edu/nineplanets/nineplanets/moon.html
http://www.fourmilab.ch/earthview/vplanet.html
http://space.jpl.nasa.gov/

HELPFUL HINTS AND DISCUSSION

Time frame: 40 minutes, or a single period
Structure: In pairs
Location: In class

For this activity, the student acting as the Earth in step 5 must be able to rotate easily, either in a chair or on the floor. It is also important in step 5 that the moon's orbit be at eye level to the student acting as the Earth. It might be helpful, though not necessary, to mark out the moon's orbit with tape on the floor prior to step 6. The circle should be about a meter (or a yard) in radius, so that several pairs of students can do the exercise simultaneously without interfering with each other.

ADAPTATIONS FOR HIGH AND LOW ACHIEVERS

High Achievers: Encourage these students to do the Extension and Follow-up Activity. You can also challenge them to connect this activity with the activity on lunar phases to conclude that, viewed from the moon, the Earth exhibits phases. They can then extend this concept to viewing any object illuminated by the Sun from any other object.

Low Achievers: Have reference books that explain the moon's orbit available for these students. They may need to do steps 4–6 more than once to understand the concept of synchronous rotation. You can pair low achievers with high achievers for this exercise.

SCORING RUBRIC

Full credit can be given to students who discover that they must rotate the moon once per orbit to keep the same face pointing toward the Earth. Extra credit can be given to students who do the Extension or Follow-up Activity. The quiz can be scored from 1 to 3 correct.

 QUIZ

1. Approximately how much of the moon's surface is ever visible from Earth?
2. Define synchronous rotation.
3. How many rotations does the moon go through each time it completes an orbit around the Earth?

Name _____   Date _____

How Does the Moon Rotate?

☀ **BEFORE YOU BEGIN** ☀

You already know that the moon orbits the Earth once every month. It is also true that the moon keeps the same face toward the Earth all the time, so we only ever see about half of the moon's surface. What you may not have realized is that put together, these two statements mean that the moon must rotate about once on its axis for every time it orbits around the Earth. That is, the moon's rotational period (the time it takes to complete one rotation about its axis) is about the same as its orbital period (the time it takes to complete one orbit). This equality of the orbital and rotational periods is called **synchronous rotation**. Synchronous rotation occurs because of subtle gravitational effects of the two objects on each other. In this activity you will simulate the moon's synchronous rotation.

 MATERIALS

- Styrofoam ball, about 3–5 inches in diameter
- Pushpin
- Wooden dowel, about $\frac{1}{2}$ inch in diameter, about 1 foot long
- Marker
- Swivel chair

 PROCEDURE

1. Insert the wooden dowel into the center of the Styrofoam ball. The dowel represents the rotational axis of the moon.

2. Hold the dowel vertically, as shown in Figure 1. Consider the point where the dowel goes into the ball as the "north pole." The point on the ball opposite the "north pole" is then the "south pole." Use a marker to draw the moon's equator as a circle halfway between the north pole and the south pole.

3. Press the pushpin into the ball to make a "mountain" on the equator as shown in Figure 1. With the marker, draw an "X" on the equator on the side of the moon opposite from the mountain. Draw a line from the mountain to the south pole.

4. One of you will be the Earth, while the other will be the moon. The "Earth" should sit in a chair that can swivel around. If no swivel chair is available, the "Earth" may sit on the floor. The partner representing Earth must be able to spin around faster than the moon revolves in its orbit. Hold the dowel vertically and line it up so that the mountain is pointing right at the Earth, as shown in Figure 2.

(continued)

How Does the Moon Rotate? *(continued)*

5. The "moon" partner should *slowly* walk around the "Earth" in a circle about 1 meter (or 1 yard) in radius, moving in a path similar to the moon's orbit. Make exactly one orbit, being sure always to keep yourself and the mountain pointing directly at the Earth. The "Earth" partner should rotate on the swivel chair many times during the time it takes the "moon" to complete the one orbit. As the "moon" moves around the orbit, notice whether or not the "Earth" appears to rotate from the "moon's" point of view, and ask the "Earth" whether or not the moon appears to rotate from his or her point of view. Enter this in the Data Collection and Analysis section.

6. The "Earth" partner should lie down on the floor with one arm raised in a fist, which will now represent the Earth. The moon partner should slowly walk around the Earth one time with the mountain pointing directly at the Earth. The partner on the floor is now playing the part of an observer at a fixed point in space neither on the Earth nor the moon. Ask this partner whether or not the moon appears to rotate from his or her point of view. This partner should carefully watch the line between the mountain and the south pole to determine this. Enter this in the Data Collection and Analysis section.

7. Now switch places and repeat steps 4–6.

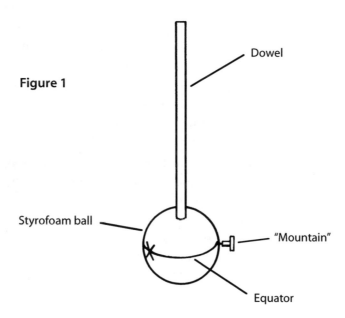

Figure 1

Dowel

Styrofoam ball

"Mountain"

Equator

(continued)

How Does the Moon Rotate? *(continued)*

Figure 2

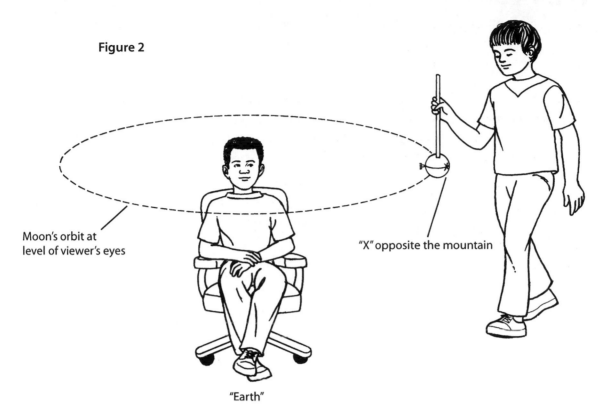

Moon's orbit at
level of viewer's eyes

"X" opposite the mountain

"Earth"

DATA COLLECTION AND ANALYSIS

In step 5, when you were playing the part of the moon, how many times did the Earth
(your partner) appear to rotate from the moon's point of view? _____

In step 5, when your partner was playing the part of the Earth, how many times did
the moon appear to rotate from the Earth's point of view? _____

In step 6, how many times did the moon appear to rotate from the point of view
of the observer at a fixed point in space? _____

(continued)

How Does the Moon Rotate? *(continued)*

 CONCLUDING QUESTIONS

1. To keep the mountain pointing at your partner, what did the moon have to do as it orbited?

    _____

    How many rotations does the moon go through during each orbit?

    _____

2. Can an observer on Earth ever see the part of the moon represented by the "X"? _____
    When an object is in synchronous orbit, about how much of the orbiting object (e.g., the moon)
    is never seen from the central object (for example, the Earth)?

    _____

3. Its synchronous orbit means that the moon always keeps the same side toward the Earth. But
    because the Earth is rotating relatively quickly, all parts of it can be seen from the moon over the
    course of a day. What would Earth's rotation period have to be for it to always show the same face
    to the moon?

    _____

EXTENSION

Imagine that you live on the side of the moon that faces the Earth. Describe how Earth's appearance would change in the sky over the course of a month. Ignore the rotation of the Earth.
(Hint: There are two things to think about. First, think about the position of the Earth in your
sky, and second, think about how you would see the Earth illuminated by the Sun. It may help
to make a sketch of the positions of Earth, moon, and Sun.)

☼ Follow-up Activity ☼

The moon is not the only object in the solar system that exhibits synchronous rotation. The
four Galilean moons of Jupiter as well as Pluto and its moon, Charon, also exhibit synchronous rotation. Look up their periods and make a chart showing the periods of all these
objects, including the moon.

EXTENSION

Long ago the moon rotated more rapidly than once each month. The process that has slowed
its rotation has also been slowing the Earth's rotation. Eventually, the Earth and moon will
both be in synchronous rotation, always keeping the same faces toward each other. Research
and write a brief report about the evidence indicating how we know that the Earth used to
rotate faster.

Observing the Sun

 INSTRUCTIONAL OBJECTIVES

Students will be able to

- construct and use a pinhole camera.
- describe the heating effect of the Sun.

 NATIONAL SCIENCE STANDARDS ADDRESSED

Students demonstrate an understanding of

- the role of the Sun as a major source of energy for phenomena on the Earth's surface.
- interaction of energy and matter.
- transfer of energy.

Students demonstrate scientific inquiry and problem-solving skills by

- identifying and controlling variables in experimental research settings.
- working individually and in teams to collect and share information and ideas.

Students demonstrate effective scientific communication by

- arguing from evidence and data.

 MATERIALS

Part A

For each group of five to seven students:

- Assorted empty cardboard boxes
- Duct tape or wide masking tape
- Meterstick or tape measure
- Scissors
- Aluminum foil
- Sewing needle
- Sheet of white paper

Part B

For each student:

- Thermometer

EXTENSION

- World Wide Web access

HELPFUL HINTS AND DISCUSSION

Time frame: 90 minutes, over several days (depending on the weather)
Structure: Part A in groups of five to seven, Part B individually
Location: Part A in class, Part B in class or at home

Supervise the students' design and construction of pinhole cameras. Stress the fact that pinhole cameras have no film—rather, that the image is projected onto a screen. Cardboard boxes should be easy to get from a local grocery store. Be sure the connections between the boxes that make up the long tube are sturdy. Also be sure that the cutout for the observer's head is sufficiently large, and is far enough from the screen to allow the observer to focus on the image (the eye should be about one foot from the screen). If your students are lucky they may be able to observe limb darkening (the face of the Sun appears darker near the edges than near the center of the circle) and sunspots.

 Be sure to remind students never to look at the Sun.

The Web sites listed in the first Extension usually have current-day images of the Sun available. In order to have professional images to which the students can compare their observations, you may want to arrange for Web access on the same day as their observations.

ADAPTATIONS FOR HIGH AND LOW ACHIEVERS

High Achievers: Encourage these students to do the Extensions and Follow-up Activity.

Low Achievers: Have reference materials available for these students. You can group these students with high achievers for Part A.

SCORING RUBRIC

Full credit can be given to students whose observations of the Sun through the pinhole camera are reasonable, and who answer the Concluding Questions correctly and in complete sentences. Extra credit can be given to students who do the Extensions or Follow-up Activity. The quiz can be scored from 1 to 4 correct.

INTERNET TIE-INS   http://www.athena.ivv.nasa.gov/curric/space/sun/index.html
http://www.azcentral.com/depts/azscience/sunchart.html
http://solar-center.stanford.edu
(See also the first Extension Activity on page 63.)

QUIZ   1. True or false: Stars and planets both give off light they generate themselves.
2. Which two gases make up most of the Sun?
3. List two ways the Sun's energy is important to life on Earth.
4. How does a pinhole camera differ from an ordinary camera?

Observing the Sun

☼ BEFORE YOU BEGIN ☼

No study of the solar system would be complete without discussing the Sun itself. The phrase "solar system" comes from *sol,* one of the many names people have given to the Sun. The Sun is a star, a sphere composed of mostly hydrogen and helium gases. Unlike planets, stars give off their own light, which comes from energy produced in their centers. The Sun is about a million miles in diameter. As stars go the Sun is quite ordinary. There are stars both hotter and cooler, bigger and smaller, brighter and fainter than the Sun. But the Sun is special because we happen to live on a planet orbiting it. The Sun is the primary source of the energy that enables life to exist on Earth.

In this activity you will observe the Sun using a simple homemade instrument called a **pinhole camera**, which allows safe viewing of the Sun's image. The pinhole camera is not like an ordinary camera. There are no lenses or mirrors, and no film. A pinhole camera directs light from each part of an object to the corresponding part of an image on a screen, as shown in Figure 1.

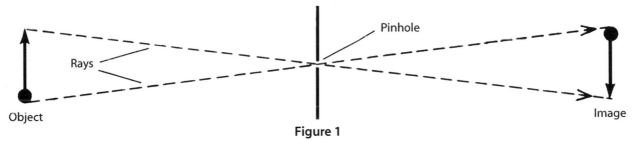

Figure 1

In addition to providing us with light, the Sun's energy drives winds and weather on Earth. In Part B of this activity you will directly observe another way in which the Sun is important for us.

MATERIALS

Part A
For each group of five to seven students:

- Assorted empty cardboard boxes
- Duct tape or wide masking tape
- Meterstick or tape measure
- Scissors

- Aluminum foil
- Sewing needle
- Sheet of white paper

Part B
For each student:
- Thermometer

EXTENSION
- World Wide Web access

(continued)

Name _____   Date _____

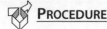 **PROCEDURE**

Part A

> 🤚 **Safety note: Never look directly at the Sun, even through the pinhole.**

1. Working in groups of five to seven students, design and build a large pinhole camera to view the Sun. One possible arrangement is shown in Figure 2, but the details of construction will depend on the available materials. Some suggestions are:

   (a) Make the pinhole about $\frac{1}{16}$ inch in diameter or smaller in the middle of one end of the camera. You may need to experiment to get just the right size and to make a clean, sharp-edged hole. One way to do this is to replace a small patch of the cardboard box with a thin, opaque material such as aluminum foil, and then poke a hole in the foil with a pointed object like a sewing needle.

   (b) Place the viewing screen (the sheet of white paper) at the opposite end of the camera, up to 10 feet away from the pinhole. At 10 feet the image of the Sun will be about 1 inch in diameter. A shorter camera will produce a smaller image.

   (c) Make a cutout so that you can put your head in the dark box to view the image of the Sun on the screen, but be sure your head will not get in the way of light going from the pinhole to the screen.

   (d) Be careful to seal off any other holes where light might enter (except, of course, the cutout for your head).

2. On a sunny day, go outdoors with your pinhole camera. Members of the group will take turns being the "observer." Everyone but the observer should support the camera and point the end with the pinhole at the Sun. The observer should place his or her head in the cutout, facing the screen. Finding the Sun may require patience. The students holding the camera may have to maneuver it a bit to get the image of the Sun on the screen. The observer should now carefully observe the image of the Sun, making particular note of how uniform or non-uniform the brightness across the face of the Sun appears, any dark areas on the Sun's surface, and whether anything appears beyond the circular edge of the Sun.

3. After getting out of the camera, the observer should record what he or she saw in the Data Collection and Analysis section.

4. Repeat steps 2 and 3 with each member of your group taking a turn as observer.

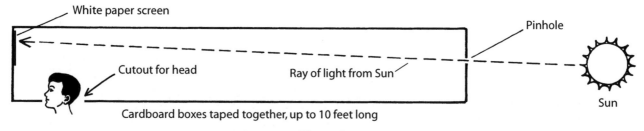

Figure 2

(continued)

Observing the Sun *(continued)*

Part B

Every thermometer has a temperature-sensing part. On an alcohol lab thermometer and on some outdoor thermometers, it's the bulb at the bottom filled with red liquid. On a digital outdoor thermometer, it's usually a small plastic probe at the end of a wire.

1. Go outdoors on a sunny day. Hold the thermometer, being careful not to touch the temperature-sensing part to anything, including yourself.
2. Stand with your back to the Sun so that the temperature-sensing part of the thermometer is in your shadow. Wait about 3 minutes and read the temperature. Record your result in the Data Collection and Analysis section. Circle either °C or °F, depending on the temperature scale of your thermometer.
3. Now hold the temperature-sensing part of the thermometer in direct sunlight. Wait about 3 minutes and read the temperature. Record your result in the Data Collection and Analysis section.
4. Calculate the change in temperature from step 2 to step 3, and record your result in the Data Collection and Analysis section.

 DATA COLLECTION AND ANALYSIS

Part A

Record your observations of the Sun here:

Part B

Temperature in shadow	_____ °C or °F
Temperature in sunlight	_____ °C or °F
Temperature change: (sunlight → shadow)	_____ °C or °F

(continued)

Observing the Sun *(continued)*

<u>EXTENSION</u>

The Sun has an 11-year cycle of "activity," as indicated by the number of sunspots, prominences, and flares. Research the solar activity cycle, and find out at what part of the cycle (peak activity, lowest activity, somewhere in the middle, etc.) your observations in Part A of this activity were done. Then visit the Web sites of some professional solar observatories, for example:

> http://www.sunspot.noao.edu/latest_solar_images.html
> http://www.bbso.njit.edu/cgi-bin/LatestImages
> http://128.171.5.17/MWLT/mwlt.html

Find images of the Sun taken as close in time as possible to your observations, preferably on the same day. Compare the features visible in the professional images to what you saw in your pinhole camera.

? CONCLUDING QUESTIONS

1. Why is a pinhole camera a safe way to observe the Sun?

   _____

   _____

2. Why is energy from the Sun important for the Earth?

   _____

   _____

3. In Part B, what direct effect of the Sun on the thermometer did you observe? Describe an indirect way (there are many!) in which the Sun accomplishes the same effect on your body.

   _____

   _____

<u>EXTENSION</u>

What types of features are visible in images of the Sun taken at professional observatories that were not visible in your observations?

☀ Follow-up Activity ☀

Many civilizations have worshipped the Sun as a god. To understand why this might be, research and write a short report on Sun-worship in at least three ancient societies. Include the name or names given to their Sun-gods, the name, location, and any physical objects (temples, monuments, statues . . .) related to these Sun-gods, and rituals meant to please these Sun-gods. Discuss similarities and differences in Sun-worship among these societies, and why societies in vastly separate parts of the world might have developed a similar worship of the Sun.

Solar Eclipses

 INSTRUCTIONAL OBJECTIVES

Students will be able to

- understand how and why eclipses of the Sun occur.
- demonstrate eclipses of the Sun.

 NATIONAL SCIENCE STANDARDS ADDRESSED

Students demonstrate an understanding of

- eclipses.
- predictable motions in the solar system.

Students demonstrate scientific inquiry and problem-solving skills by

- identifying variables in experimental and non-experimental settings.
- using evidence from reliable sources to develop models.
- using previously learned concepts to explain observed phenomena.

Students demonstrate effective scientific communication by

- arguing from evidence and data.
- representing data in multiple ways.

 MATERIALS

Part A

For each pair of students:

- Ping-Pong ball
- Baseball
- Table
- Meterstick or yardstick
- Ruler marked in millimeters
- Adhesive putty

Part B

For the class as a whole:

- A tall sheet of cardboard, as from an appliance box
- Tape measure
- Chalk or removable tape
- 5 sheets of 8.5" × 11" white paper
- Felt-tip marker

HELPFUL HINTS AND DISCUSSION

Time frame: Two periods
Structure: Part A in pairs, Part B as a class
Location: Part A in class or at home, Part B in class

This activity is relatively long. You may choose to do Part A, Part B, or both. In any of these cases the Before You Begin section is appropriate preparation. If you choose to do only one part, a single period of instruction will suffice.

For Part A, the students will be simulating an eclipse with a nearby small object eclipsing a larger, more distant one. The students are asked to measure the diameters of the Ping-Pong ball and the baseball. They can either measure them directly with the ruler, or wrap a tape measure around the widest part of each to measure the circumference. They can then calculate the diameter:

$$\text{diameter} = \text{circumference}/3.14$$

For Part B, students will examine the concept of a shadow cone using a barrier to block their view of some classmates. If a sheet of cardboard is used as the visual barrier, it should be taller than the students to completely block their view. If the class is large, don't put more than 13 students on each of the two lines. Assign some of the remaining students to construct the visual barrier, hold the barrier upright in place, and draw chalk lines on the ground or tape the ground as described. If the class is small, some students will have to perform more than one task. During the preparation phase, to save time, the group working on the visual barrier can work separately from the group laying out the marks on the ground. When students draw the two parallel lines on the ground, make sure they line up like this: ========= and are not skewed like this: ————— . Steps 4–8 will be performed at least twice; the second trial is to give those initially on the Sun side a chance to observe from the Earth side. If some students have been occupied with other tasks for the first two trials, do a third trial with these students on the Earth-side line so that they may carry out their observations.

ADAPTATIONS FOR HIGH AND LOW ACHIEVERS

High Achievers: Encourage these students to do the Extensions and Follow-up Activities.

Low Achievers: Have reference books and eclipse geometry diagrams for these students to consult. You can pair low achievers with high achievers for Part A.

SCORING RUBRIC

Full credit can be given to students who find approximately correct values for the sizes, distances, and ratios in Part A, and/or who participate fully in the whole-class exercise in Part B. The quiz can be scored from 1 to 5 correct.

  INTERNET TIE-INS   http://sunearth.gsfc.nasa.gov/eclipse/SEnovice.html

QUIZ   1. A solar eclipse can only happen at what phase of the moon?
2. Can a solar eclipse occur every month? Explain your answer.
3. The apparent size of the moon in the sky is (smaller than, larger than, or the same as) the apparent size of the Sun.
4. Can anyone on the daytime side of the Earth see a solar eclipse when it occurs?
5. One way of describing a solar eclipse is to say that a part of the Earth is in the moon's _____.

Solar Eclipses

☼ BEFORE YOU BEGIN ☼

In its monthly orbit around the Earth, the moon goes through its cycle of phases from new to full and back to new again. Usually, the phase we call the new moon is seen when the moon is nearly between the Earth and the Sun. But the moon is not *exactly* between, because its orbit around the Sun is slightly tilted relative to the Earth's orbit, as shown in Figure 1. This tilt means that twice each month the moon crosses the plane of Earth's orbit. If the moon is in its new phase at the same time it is crossing the Earth's orbit, then it *is* lined up exactly between Earth and the Sun. When this happens the moon completely covers the Sun, creating a **total eclipse** of the Sun, or, **total solar eclipse**.

The Sun is much larger in diameter than the moon. In fact, it is 400 times larger. How then can the moon completely cover the Sun, when the Sun is so much larger? By a wonderful coincidence, the Sun happens to be 400 times as far away from Earth as the moon! This means that the Sun and the moon appear to be very nearly the *same size in the sky*, so that the moon is able to just barely cover the Sun.

Another way to describe an eclipse is to say that the moon's shadow falls on the Earth, as shown in Figure 2. Observers in the area where the moon's shadow falls cannot see the Sun. This area is very small, only a few tens of kilometers wide. As Earth rotates and the moon moves in its orbit, the shadow moves across the face of the Earth and traces out a path that can be thousands of kilometers long. Only observers along that path will see the Sun completely covered by the moon. At any one location this complete coverage lasts only a few minutes, seven at the most. At many locations the alignment of the Sun, moon, and Earth are not perfect. Only part of the surface of the Sun is blocked, and a *partial* solar eclipse is seen.

During a solar eclipse, when the part of the Sun we normally see is covered, faint outer portions of the Sun's atmosphere become visible. In particular, the **corona**, which means "crown," can be seen as a faint, ghostly halo around the Sun. Expeditions to areas where solar eclipses can be seen are an important part of modern solar research.

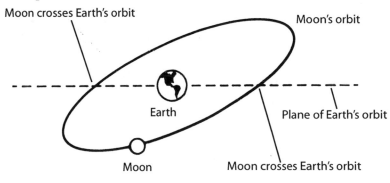

Figure 1 (not to scale)

(continued)

Solar Eclipses (continued)

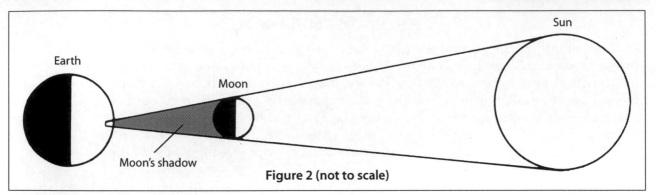

Earth

Moon

Sun

Moon's shadow

Figure 2 (not to scale)

 MATERIALS

Part A

- Ping-Pong ball
- Baseball
- Table
- Meterstick or yardstick
- Ruler marked in millimeters
- Adhesive putty

Part B

- A tall sheet of cardboard, as from an appliance box
- Tape measure
- Chalk or removable tape
- 5 sheets of 8.5" × 11" white paper
- Felt-tip marker

 PROCEDURE

Part A

1. Set the meterstick flat on the table so that the "0" end hangs slightly off the end of the table, as shown in Figure 3.
2. Stick a small lump of adhesive putty on the top surface of the meterstick at the 40-cm mark, and stick the Ping-Pong ball onto the adhesive putty. The center of the Ping-Pong ball should be at the 40-cm mark.

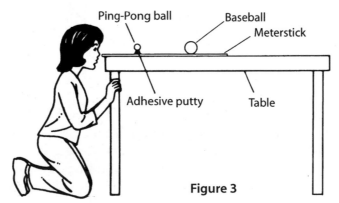

Ping-Pong ball

Baseball

Meterstick

Adhesive putty

Table

Figure 3

(continued)

Solar Eclipses *(continued)*

3. Position yourself in a sitting or kneeling position at the end of the table so that your eye level is just above the table and you can sight along the meterstick. Your eye should be just above the "0" mark on the meterstick.

4. Have your partner place the baseball on top of the meterstick with its center at the 50-cm mark. Adjust your head position so that the Ping-Pong ball appears directly in front of (centered on) the baseball. Observe which ball appears larger, and record your observations in the Data Collection and Analysis section.

5. While you sight along the meterstick, move your head sideways or up and down if necessary to keep the image of the Ping-Pong ball centered on the image of the baseball. Then have your partner move the baseball away from you along the top of the meterstick. Tell your partner to stop at the point where you see that the Ping-Pong ball just barely covers the baseball. You now have a "total eclipse of the baseball." Record the distance from your eye to the center of the baseball in the Data Collection and Analysis section.

6. Measure the diameters of the Ping-Pong ball and the baseball in millimeters and record them in the Data Collection and Analysis section.

7. Calculate and record the ratio of the baseball's diameter to the Ping-Pong ball's diameter, and the ratio of the baseball's distance from your eye to the Ping-Pong ball's distance from your eye.

Part B

Part B is to be done as a class in the schoolyard or gymnasium. Your teacher will assign you to one or more tasks.

1. Construct a visual barrier 5 feet wide and 6 feet high out of cardboard or other easily available material. Write the word "SUN" in large letters on each of the five sheets of white paper.

2. Select an open area of the schoolyard or gymnasium. Use the chalk or removable tape to make lines and marks on the ground as in the description that follows. Draw two parallel lines 25 feet long and 18 feet apart. Find the midpoint of each of these lines and mark it with an "X." Starting at the midpoint of each of the parallel lines, mark an "X" on each line every 2 feet out to both ends. Label one of these lines "Sun side" and the other "Earth side."

3. Draw or tape a line connecting the midpoints of the parallel lines. Make an "X" at the midpoint of this connecting line. Place the visual barrier on this mark, with the 6-foot dimension vertical. Be sure that the barrier is aligned parallel to the two lines drawn in step 2. At this point the schoolyard or gymnasium should look like Figure 4.

4. If the visual barrier is not self-supporting, two students should stand on opposite sides of the barrier, with backs against the barrier to hold it up.

5. A student should stand on each of the "X" marks made in step 2, directly facing the other line. It's OK to have students missing at the ends of the lines, but all positions near the middle of the lines must be occupied. Count the total number of students on the Sun-side line and have everyone on the Earth-side line record this number in the Data Collection and Analysis section, Part B.

6. The middle five students (the student on the midpoint mark plus two students on either side) on the Sun-side line should now hold up the sheets of paper marked "SUN."

(continued)

Solar Eclipses (continued)

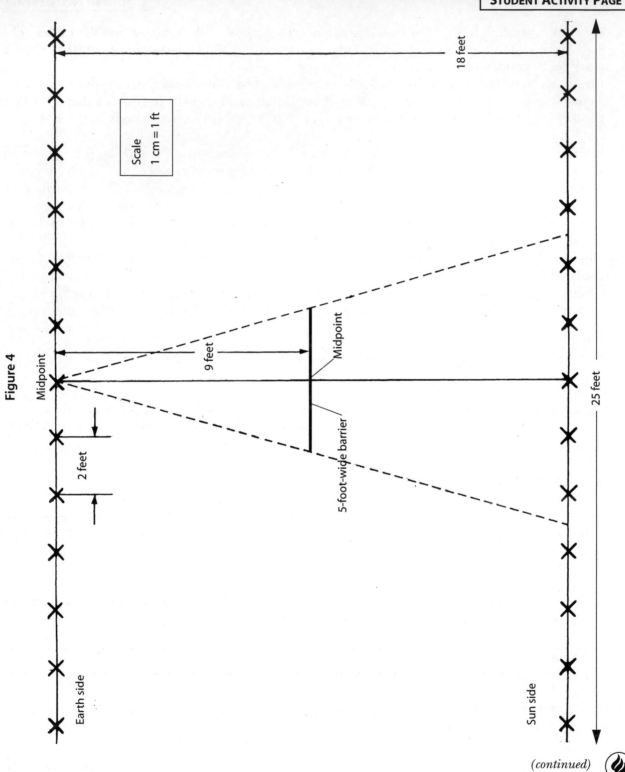

Figure 4

Scale
1 cm = 1 ft

18 feet

25 feet

Midpoint

9 feet

Midpoint

5-foot-wide barrier

2 feet

Earth side

Sun side

(continued)

Solar Eclipses *(continued)*

7. Each student in the Earth-side row should count the number of students he or she can see on the Sun-side line who are holding sheets of paper marked "SUN." Each student should record this number in the Data Collection and Analysis section.

8. All students on the Earth-side line should compare notes. They should record directly onto Figure 4 the number of sheets marked "Sun" each of them saw. Record these numbers just above the "X" representing each Earth-side student.

9. Students in the Earth-side and Sun-side lines should exchange places and repeat steps 4–8.

DATA COLLECTION AND ANALYSIS

Part A

In step 4, which ball appears larger? _____

Distance to the Ping-Pong ball	__40__	cm
Distance to the baseball when fully covered by the Ping-Pong ball	_____	cm
Diameter of Ping-Pong ball	_____	mm
Diameter of baseball	_____	mm
(size of baseball)/(size of Ping-Pong ball)	_____	(decimal fraction)
(distance to baseball)/(distance to Ping-Pong ball)	_____	(decimal fraction)

EXTENSION

Look up the diameters of the Sun and the moon in km and their average distances from Earth in km. Verify that the ratio of their distances from Earth is the same as the ratio of their diameters.

Part B

Total number of students on the Sun-side line: _____

How many students can you see who are holding sheets of paper marked "Sun"? _____

Record the number of sheets marked "Sun" for all students in your Earth-side group directly onto Figure 4.

CONCLUDING QUESTIONS

1. Under the conditions in Part A, step 4, if the Ping-Pong ball represents the moon and the baseball represents the Sun, can there be a total solar eclipse? Why or why not?

_____

_____

(continued)

Solar Eclipses *(continued)*

2. At the end of step 5, how does the ratio of the baseball's diameter to the Ping-Pong ball's diameter compare with the ratio of the distance between your eye and the baseball, and the distance between your eye and the Ping-Pong ball? How does this explain the existence of solar eclipses?

    _____

    _____

3. How many students in your group saw no students on the Sun side holding a sheet marked "Sun"? _____ How does this relate to the number of people on Earth who can observe a total solar eclipse when one occurs?

    _____

    _____

4. What pattern do you notice in the distribution of numbers you wrote on the Earth-side line on Figure 4? What kind of "eclipse" did those who wrote a number other than 0 or 5 experience?

    _____

    _____

    _____

EXTENSION

Make a graph of the numbers recorded by the students in your Earth-side group in step 6 as a function of position along the line.

☼ Follow-up Activities ☼

1. Search the World Wide Web for images of total solar eclipses. Print out some and make a poster for your classroom. Include a drawing of how the Sun, moon, and Earth are lined up in a solar eclipse.

2. Find out when the next total solar eclipse will be visible from a location near you.

3. The moon has not always orbited the Earth at its present distance. Hundreds of millions of years ago, the moon orbited significantly closer to the Earth. Describe how this would have affected the area on Earth over which an eclipse was visible, and how it would have affected the duration of an eclipse. What will happen hundreds of millions of years from now when the moon is significantly farther from the Earth?

EXTENSION

The moon's orbit around the Earth is not a circle, but an ellipse. Therefore, the moon's distance from the Earth varies a little, so its apparent size must also vary. When the moon is at its farthest from the Earth, it appears too small to completely cover the Sun. An eclipse that happens then will not be total, but a ring of sunlight will show around the moon. This is called an **annular** (not "annual"!) eclipse. Find a picture of an annular eclipse and show it to the class.

Volcanoes

 INSTRUCTIONAL OBJECTIVES

Students will be able to
- describe the locations of volcanoes in the solar system.
- describe the various kinds of volcanoes found in the solar system.

 NATIONAL SCIENCE STANDARDS ADDRESSED

Students demonstrate an understanding of
- origin and evolution of the Earth system.
- evolution of the solar system.
- chemical reactions.

Students demonstrate scientific inquiry and problem-solving skills by
- identifying variables in experimental and non-experimental settings.
- working in teams to collect and share information and ideas.

Students demonstrate effective scientific communication by
- arguing from evidence and data.

 MATERIALS

For each group of two or three students:
- Small (about 9-inch) pie tin, baking dish, or roasting pan
- Plastic drinking straw with flexible tip
- 1 tsp baking soda
- $\frac{1}{8}$ cup white vinegar
- Adhesive tape (transparent, vinyl electrical, etc.)
- Spoon
- 1 to $1\frac{1}{2}$ cups uncooked farina
- Small funnel, beaker, or graduated cylinder
- Pen or pencil
- Ruler or straightedge
- $8\frac{1}{2}" \times 11"$ sheet of white paper

HELPFUL HINTS AND DISCUSSION

Time frame: 40 minutes, or a single period
Structure: In groups of two or three students
Location: In class

If you have funnels small enough to fit into a straw, supply these to the students. Otherwise, have them use a small beaker or graduated cylinder and have them very carefully pour the vinegar into the straw. You may want to have them practice this with plain water after completing step 1 but before doing step 2.

Farina is specified in the materials list to simulate the crust through which the magma pushes. You may want to try other loose, granular materials such as cornmeal or fine sand. Different materials may yield "volcanoes" with a variety of physical characteristics.

ADAPTATIONS FOR HIGH AND LOW ACHIEVERS

High Achievers: Encourage these students to do the Extension and Follow-up Activity.

Low Achievers: Have reference materials available for these students. You also can pair them with high achievers for the exercise.

SCORING RUBRIC

Full credit can be given to students whose volcanoes appear reasonable, and who answer the Concluding Questions correctly and in complete sentences. Extra credit can be awarded to students who do the Extension or Follow-up Activity. The quiz can be scored from 1 to 4 correct.

 INTERNET TIE-INS   http://volcano.und.nodak.edu/vwdocs/planet_volcano/other_worlds.html

 QUIZ
1. Define magma.
2. How is Earth's crust different from the crust on other terrestrial planets?
3. On which planets do we find evidence of volcanic activity?
4. On which bodies in the solar system is there clear evidence of current volcanic activity?

Volcanoes

☼ BEFORE YOU BEGIN ☼

The Earth's crust sits above a hot layer of rock called the **mantle**. Where the crust meets the mantle, the temperature is high enough that the solid crust turns into molten rock called **magma**. In some places the crust is thin and weak or is located over especially hot spots in the mantle. In these places, magma can flow up through and on top of the crust. We call this a **volcano**. On Earth there are several different kinds of volcanoes. The type of volcano depends on the path the magma takes through the crust, on the magma's chemical makeup, and on the kind of rock and landscape where the magma erupts. The Earth is special among the terrestrial planets. Its crust is split into several plates that float and move over the mantle. As a plate moves over a hot spot, a string of volcanoes will form. The Hawaiian Islands are an example of such a **volcano chain**.

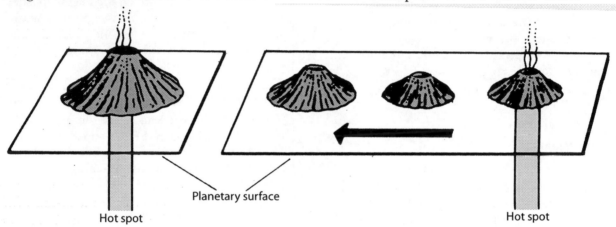

Planetary surface

Hot spot

Hot spot

Figure 1a: Crust stationary over mantle   **Figure 1b: Plate moving over mantle**

But far from being a unique feature of Earth, volcanoes are common through much of the solar system. On Mars and Venus, which also have volcanoes, the planetary crust is not fractured into moving plates. In this case, single very large volcanoes will build up from many eruptions in the same place over millions of years. Olympus Mons on Mars, at 27 km high, is the largest volcano in the solar system. Though Earth certainly has active volcanoes, and the volcanoes on Venus seen on radar images *may* be active, Mars' volcanoes are all long dead. Mercury never had volcanoes at all.

Because they do not have solid surfaces, the gas giant planets cannot have volcanoes, but their moons (which do have solid surfaces) can! Tiny Io, a moon of Jupiter, is the most volcanically active place in the solar system. Images taken by the *Voyager* spacecraft in the 1980's showed active eruptions, spewing colorful sulfur compounds coming from Io's interior. Even more unusual is the evidence for past volcanic activity on Neptune's moon, Triton, on which we see frozen "lakes" of erupted volcanic material, probably composed of frozen methane, ammonia, and water ice. Though Triton's volcanoes are not active now, at some time in the past there must have been a source of internal heating. It is too cold inside Triton to melt rock, so volcanoes there did not produced magma as they do on Earth.

(continued)

Volcanoes (continued)

 ### MATERIALS

For each group of two or three students:

- Small (about 9-inch) pie tin, baking dish, or roasting pan
- Plastic drinking straw with flexible tip
- 1 tsp baking soda
- $\frac{1}{8}$ cup white vinegar
- Adhesive tape (transparent, vinyl electrical, etc.)
- Spoon

- 1 to $1\frac{1}{2}$ cups uncooked farina (Cream of Wheat-type cereal)
- Small funnel, beaker, or graduated cylinder
- Pen or pencil
- Ruler or straightedge
- $8\frac{1}{2}$" × 11" sheet of white paper

PROCEDURE

In this activity you will make a model volcano in which the energy is provided by a chemical reaction, rather than by rising magma. Baking soda and vinegar combine to make carbon dioxide, which pushes up through the overlying material.

1. Using the pencil and ruler, divide the sheet of paper into three approximately equal sections. Label the sections "Step 4," "Step 5," and "Step 6."
2. Bend the drinking straw at its flexible point to approximately a right angle. Tape the straw to the bottom of the pan so that the short part points upward near the rim of the pan, as shown in Figure 2. Have the long end of the straw stop near the middle of the pan. Shorten it if necessary.
3. Place the teaspoon of baking soda in a small mound covering the opening of the long side of the straw in the bottom of the pan. The pile should be about $\frac{1}{4}$ to $\frac{3}{8}$ inch high and about $\frac{3}{4}$ to 1 inch in diameter. Without disturbing the mound of baking soda, spread the farina around the bottom of the pan until the top of the farina is level with the top of the baking soda. Cover the entire surface with an additional $\frac{1}{4}$ to $\frac{3}{8}$ inch of farina.
4. With the pan on a level surface, pour a small amount (about a teaspoon) of vinegar into the straw using the funnel, beaker, or graduated cylinder. Be careful to get all the vinegar into the straw, and spill as little as possible onto the farina. Observe what happens in the first 2–3 seconds and record your observation in the Data Collection and Analysis section. Wait about 2 minutes, and sketch what you see on the sheet of drawing paper in the section labeled "Step 4."
5. Pour a much larger amount of vinegar into the straw, leaving about a teaspoon of vinegar unused from your original $\frac{1}{8}$ cup. Again observe what happens in the first 2–3 seconds and record your observation in the Data Collection and Analysis section. Wait about 5 minutes and sketch what you see on the sheet of drawing paper in the section labeled "Step 5."
6. Pour the last teaspoon of vinegar in the straw. Wait about 10 minutes and sketch what you see on the sheet of drawing paper in the section labeled "Step 6."

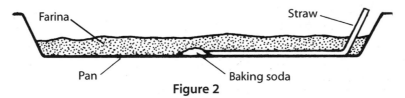

Figure 2

(continued)

Volcanoes (continued)

DATA COLLECTION AND ANALYSIS

Step 4 observation:

The first 2–3 seconds: _____

Step 5 observation:

The first 2–3 seconds: _____

CONCLUDING QUESTIONS

1. Based on your observations, describe how a volcanic eruption changes the appearance of an initially flat surface. _____

   _____

2. Is your volcano, repeatedly erupting in the same spot, more like volcanoes in the Hawaiian chain on Earth or like Olympus Mons on Mars? Explain your answer. _____

   _____

3. How do you think your volcano would have behaved if you had used chemicals that released more energy than the vinegar and baking soda? _____ .

   Less energy? _____

   What if the overlying material were much denser? _____

4. Are the volcanic forms on other solar system objects similar to those on Earth? Why or why not?

   _____

   _____

EXTENSION

The extent of volcanic activity on a terrestrial planet is related to how much internal heat it contains, which in turn is related to its size. Think about this idea and use it to explain the current level of volcanic activity (or lack of it) on the four terrestrial planets.

☼ Follow-up Activities ☼

1. Search the World Wide Web for sites about volcanoes in the solar system. Make a poster with images of these volcanoes. Include on your poster information such as: the planet with the most volcanoes, the largest volcano, the farthest volcano from the Sun, and other interesting facts. A good starting point is: http://volcano.und.nodak.edu/

2. Research the different kinds of volcanoes on Earth. Write a brief paper describing their different causes and shapes, giving examples of each kind.

Impact Craters: Look Out Below!

 INSTRUCTIONAL OBJECTIVES

Students will be able to

- understand how impact craters are formed in the solar system.
- demonstrate the formation of impact craters.

 NATIONAL SCIENCE STANDARDS ADDRESSED

Students demonstrate an understanding of

- evolution of the solar system.
- Earth's history.
- kinetic energy.

Students demonstrate scientific inquiry and problem-solving skills by

- identifying and controlling variables in an experimental setting.
- working in teams to collect and share information and ideas.

Students demonstrate effective scientific communication by

- arguing from evidence and data.
- representing data and results in multiple ways.

 MATERIALS

For each group of two or three students:

- White flour, about 2–3 lbs
- Powdered cocoa, about $\frac{1}{4}$ cup
- Tray, box, or large clear-plastic storage container, about 12" × 18," with sides several inches high
- Large plastic garbage bag
- Fine strainer or sifter
- Meterstick
- Ruler
- 3 identical marbles
- 3 sheets of plain 8.5" × 11" drawing paper for each student

For each student doing the Extensions:

- 2 sheets of graph paper
- 3 round objects of similar size (1–2 cm diameter) but different mass (e.g., plastic, aluminum, steel)

HELPFUL HINTS AND DISCUSSION

Time frame: 40 minutes, or a single period
Structure: In groups of two or three students
Location: In class

In this activity, students will drop marbles into flour to simulate the formation of craters in the solar system. This activity might be messy, but students will enjoy doing it. Flour is probably the easiest material to obtain, but fine, clean sand will also do nicely. The box for the activity should be at least several inches high, to minimize the mess. A small carton with sides cut down or the top of a copier-paper box would be about right. If the box is lined with a plastic garbage bag the mess will be easier to dispose of. The flour should be about 2–3 inches deep; the amount students will need will depend on the size of the box. You should experiment in advance with how tightly to pack the flour down. The top layer needs to be a very contrasting color. Powdered cocoa works well, as does powdered instant coffee (not crystals). After a few impacts, the flour will need to be mixed (the dark surface material doesn't really change the color of the flour noticeably) and smoothed. Then another layer of dark material can be placed on top for more impacts. Do the activity outdoors if possible. If you do it indoors, it is important that the students clean up thoroughly to avoid attracting pests. Have several plastic trash bags with twist-ties available to dispose of the flour properly.

For the first Extension, provide the students with appropriate round objects of about the same size but of three very different masses. These may be of differing materials, or some may be hollow while others are solid. The idea is to make the result of each impact distinct from the others, even though the objects are dropped from the same height.

The idea of an asteroid or comet hitting Earth has been in the news recently, as well as in several Hollywood and TV movies. A Web site for teachers about this issue is found at http://www.aspsky.org/html/tnl/23/23.html.

ADAPTATIONS FOR HIGH AND LOW ACHIEVERS

High Achievers: Encourage these students to do the Extensions and Follow-up Activities.

Low Achievers: Review the concept of kinetic energy for these students. They can work with high achievers for the activity.

SCORING RUBRIC

Full credit can be given to students who draw their craters accurately and who answer the Concluding Questions correctly and in complete sentences. Extra credit can be given to students who complete any Extensions or Follow-up Activities. The quiz can be scored from 1 to 4 correct.

  INTERNET TIE-INS   http://seds.lpl.arizona.edu/seds/chapters/css/space101/Impact/Impact.html

QUIZ   1. What evidence do we have that craters are common in the solar system?
2. When was cratering most intense in the solar system's history?
3. Why are previous impacts not obvious on some solar system bodies?
4. True or False: The size of a crater depends on the kinetic energy of the object that hits the surface.

Name _____   Date _____

Impact Craters: Look Out Below!

☀ BEFORE YOU BEGIN ☀

Four and a half billion years ago, the solar system was a dangerous place. After the planets had formed and cooled, there were a great many leftover pieces that had not been incorporated into planets or moons. These leftover objects frequently collided with the larger bodies, leaving craters as evidence. Every solid surface in the solar system bears these scars. Some bodies, like the moon and Mercury, are heavily pockmarked with craters, since not much has happened to these objects since the time of the cratering. On other solar system bodies, however, cratering is not so obvious. Water, weather, and motion of the Earth's crust have smeared away most of Earth's craters. On Jupiter's moon, Io, material from active volcanoes has covered old craters.

Nowadays, things have quieted down considerably. Nevertheless, small objects remain on the loose in the solar system. There is always a chance (though quite small) that a planet or moon will be hit.

Figure 1 shows the structure of a typical crater. The size of an impact crater depends on the **kinetic energy** of the incoming object, which increases with both the object's mass and its velocity. Remember that the higher the distance an object is dropped from, the more kinetic energy it will have when it hits.

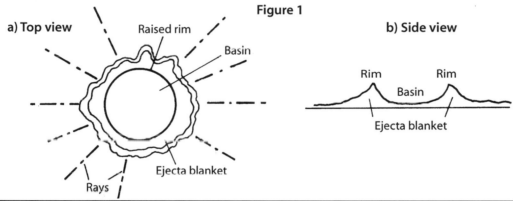

Figure 1

a) Top view — Raised rim, Basin, Ejecta blanket, Rays

b) Side view — Rim, Basin, Rim, Ejecta blanket

MATERIALS

For each group of two or three students:

- White flour, about 2–3 lbs
- Powdered cocoa, about $\frac{1}{4}$ cup
- Tray, box, or large clear-plastic storage container, about 12" × 18," with sides several inches high
- Large plastic garbage bag

- Fine strainer or sifter
- Meterstick
- Ruler
- 3 identical marbles
- 3 sheets of plain 8.5" × 11" drawing paper for each student

For each student doing the Extensions:

- 2 sheets of graph paper
- 3 round objects of similar size (1–2 cm diameter) but different mass (e.g., plastic, aluminum, steel)

(continued)

Name _____ Date _____

 PROCEDURE

1. Line the box with the garbage bag so that cleanup will be easier. Pour the flour slowly into the box to a depth of 5 to 8 cm. Shake the box back and forth horizontally to level the surface, and tap the box on the ground a few times to pack the flour down a bit. Do not press on the surface of the flour.

2. Put some powdered cocoa in the strainer, and sift some cocoa onto the surface of the flour, completely covering the white color of the flour.

3. One member of your group should drop a marble into the box from a height of about $\frac{1}{2}$ meter. Leave the marble in place. Each member of the group should examine the resulting crater closely and sketch the crater on a sheet of drawing paper. Draw views from the top and from the side, label the sheet with the height from which you dropped the marble, and label the features of the crater.

4. Have each member of the group measure the diameter of the crater basin, and the length of the longest ray measured from the center of the crater. Record these values in Table 1 in the Data Collection and Analysis section.

5. Sift a little more cocoa over the surface to cover any flour that was exposed. Another member of your group should drop a second marble from a height of $\frac{1}{4}$ meter onto an undisturbed part of the surface in the box. Each student should make and record the measurements described in step 4.

6. Again, sift a little more cocoa over the surface to cover any flour that was exposed. A member of your group should drop the third marble from a height of 1 meter onto an undisturbed part of the surface in the box. Each group member should make the measurements described in step 4.

7. Clean up thoroughly (unless you are doing the Extension below)!

EXTENSION

Mix the flour in the box with the ruler to distribute the dark powder evenly. The flour will be only slightly darker than it was before. Prepare the surface again as in steps 1 and 2. Repeat steps 3 to 7 of the main activity, but instead of varying the height from which the object is dropped, use three objects of very different masses and drop them all from the same height, say, 1 meter. All three objects will therefore hit the surface with the same velocity. Record your data in Table 2 in the Data Collection and Analysis section.

 DATA COLLECTION AND ANALYSIS

Convert your measurements to cm if necessary.

Table 1

Height Above Box (m)	Crater Diameter (cm)	Length of Longest Ray (cm)
0.25		
0.5		
1		

(continued)

Impact Craters: Look Out Below! *(continued)*

EXTENSION

Make a graph of the length of the longest ray versus the height from which the marble was dropped. Put the drop height on the horizontal axis, and the ray length on the vertical axis.

Table 2

Object	Crater Diameter (cm)	Length of Longest Ray (cm)
lightest		
medium weight		
heaviest		

EXTENSION

Make a graph of the length of the longest ray versus the weight of the object that was dropped. Use labels "light," "medium," and "heavy" on the horizontal axis, and the ray length on the vertical axis.

CONCLUDING QUESTIONS

1. Do your craters show all the features expected in an impact crater? If not, why not?

   _____

   _____

2. How does the diameter of a crater change as the impact energy increases?

   _____

   _____

3. How does the length of the longest ray change as impact energy increases?

   _____

   _____

EXTENSION

1. How does the appearance of a crater change as the mass of the impacting body increases?

   _____

   _____

(continued)

Impact Craters: Look Out Below! *(continued)*

☼ Follow-up Activities ☼

1. Here is a crater experiment you can do at home the next time you make pancakes or bake a cake. After you prepare the batter, drop small edible objects into it, one at a time, from a variety of heights. You can use blueberries, raisins, or chocolate chips. Watch what happens after impact. Be sure to watch for long enough to come to a final conclusion. Compare this to what you observed in the activity on the previous page.

2. Explore the World Wide Web to find images of craters on as many planets and moons as you can. Print out the images and make a collage for your classroom.

3. The Earth's atmosphere and life have erased or hidden evidence of the many impact craters on its surface. Visit the Web site at
   http://gdcinfo.agg.emr.ca/toc.html?/crater/world_craters.html
   and explore impact craters on Earth. Write a report or make a collage about terrestrial impact craters.

4. Rent a video of a recent Earth-impact movie. Write a short commentary on the science in the movie—did the writers and producers of the movie get it right?

Comets: Dirty Snowballs

 INSTRUCTIONAL OBJECTIVES

Students will be able to
- describe the nature and behavior of comets.
- understand and demonstrate why a comet's tail always points away from the Sun.

 NATIONAL SCIENCE STANDARDS ADDRESSED

Students demonstrate an understanding of
- evolution of the solar system.

Students demonstrate scientific inquiry and problem-solving skills by
- using relevant concepts to explain phenomena.
- using evidence from reliable sources to develop descriptions, explanations, and models.

Students demonstrate effective scientific communication by
- arguing from evidence and data.

 MATERIALS

For each pair of students:

Part A
- 3 small, good quality plastic garbage bags, preferably clear (about 8-gallon size)
- Brick or disk of dry ice, about 6–8 ounces
- Hammer to crush dry ice
- ½–1 cup of water
- A few teaspoons of fine dirt (from the schoolyard is fine)
- A few ounces of cola soft drink (flat is OK)
- A pair of thick insulated winter gloves
- Folded newspaper to hold finished comet

Part B
- Styrofoam ball about 3–4 inches in diameter
- Several 1-ft lengths of ¼- to ½-inch ribbon
- Thumbtacks
- Hair dryer or electric fan

 INTERNET TIE-INS

http://oposite.stsci.edu/pubinfo/subject.html#Comets
http://www.seasky.org/sky31.html
http:/www.tui.edu/STO/SolSys/Comets/Comets.html

HELPFUL HINTS AND DISCUSSION

Time frame: 40 minutes, or a single period
Structure: In pairs
Location: In class

Make the comets early in the period to allow sufficient time for them to "evolve." They will melt a little and sublime a little. There may be occasional spurts of gas escaping. Make sure students notice these occurrences.

It is important to instruct students in proper precautions for handling dry ice. Be sure to tell them not to touch it with bare skin. Students should wear thick insulated gloves when handling their comets. You can ask them a day ahead to bring in winter gloves. Insulated, non-porous gloves are best. Avoid cotton or plain wool gloves. The plastic bags in which students make their comets should be good quality. If the bag tears and the liquid pours out, the students will likely not be able to form a ball that will stick together.

If possible, practice making your own comet prior to doing this activity in class.

ADAPTATIONS FOR HIGH AND LOW ACHIEVERS

High Achievers: Encourage high achievers to do the Extension and Follow-up Activities.
Low Achievers: Review relevant material. Have reference materials about comets available. Pair these students with high achievers.

SCORING RUBRIC

Give full credit to students who make a comet as well as they can, and who answer the Concluding Questions accurately and in complete sentences. Extra credit can be given to students who complete the Extension or Follow-up Activities. The quiz can be scored from 1 to 4 correct.

 QUIZ
1. What period in the solar system's history does a comet represent?
2. What are the names of the two regions comets come from, and where is each located?
3. Name and describe the two kinds of comet tails.
4. True or false: In its orbit, a comet always travels head first.

Name _____ Date _____

Comets: Dirty Snowballs

☼ **BEFORE YOU BEGIN** ☼

The stars in the night sky seem unchanging. The constellations your parents and grandparents knew are the same ones you can see tonight. The stable orbits of the planets carry them around the sky in predictable ways. Everything is orderly. But once in a while, something spectacular appears. A **comet**, a leftover scrap from the early formation of the solar system, blazes in the sky for a few weeks or months. Perhaps you saw Comet Hyakutake in 1995, or Comet Hale-Bopp in 1996. Extending outward from the bright **head** of the comet, the magnificent **tail** can stretch halfway across the sky. No wonder comets have been regarded with fear, awe, and suspicion throughout history.

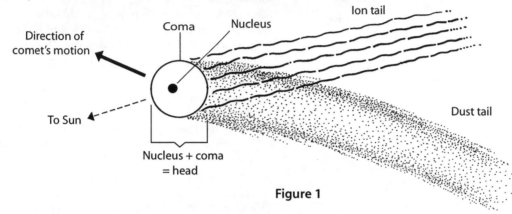

Figure 1

Far from the Sun, the comet is dark. It has only a **nucleus,** a few kilometers across, which is an icy mass mixed with rock and dust. The frozen gases in the ice include water, carbon dioxide, ammonia, and some organic compounds. As the comet approaches the Sun, the **coma** and the **tails** develop, as shown in Figure 1. The Sun's radiation heats the ices on the surface of the nucleus, but instead of melting into liquid, the ices *sublime* directly from a solid to a gas. Solar radiation then makes the gas glow. Some of the glowing gas forms the *coma*, which surrounds and hides the nucleus. The rest of the gas streams back behind the comet, always in a direction opposite the Sun, forming the **ion tail**, which is often clumpy and bluish in color. The ice on the comet is mixed with dust and broken pieces of rock. This material is released as the ices sublime, forming the **dust tail**. The dust tail, too, points generally away from the Sun. But in contrast to the ion tail, the dust tail is smooth and has a gently curving shape. It appears yellowish because the dust particles reflect light from the Sun. Whether or not a comet has both kinds of tails depends on the amounts of ice and dust it contains. Comet tails can stretch for many millions of miles across space.

Comets come from two regions far out in the solar system. One region, called the Kuiper Belt, contains many thousands of comets, and lies just beyond the orbits of Neptune and Pluto. The other, containing many millions of comets, is called the Oort Cloud, and extends in a spherical halo around the solar system, one third of the way to the nearest star beyond the solar system. While they are so far from the Sun, these comets are invisible. It is only when their orbits are jostled, perhaps by colliding with each other, that they move in toward the Sun and we can see them.

(continued)

Name _____   Date _____

Comets: Dirty Snowballs *(continued)*

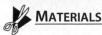 MATERIALS

Part A

- 3 small, good quality plastic garbage bags, preferably clear (about 8-gallon size)
- Brick or disk of dry ice, about 6–8 ounces
- Hammer to crush dry ice
- $\frac{1}{2}$–1 cup of water
- A few teaspoons of fine dirt (from the school-yard is fine)

- A few ounces of cola soft drink (does not need to be fresh)
- A pair of thick insulated winter gloves
- A folded newspaper on which to place the finished comet

Part B

- Styrofoam ball about 3–4 inches in diameter
- Several 1-ft lengths of $\frac{1}{4}$- to $\frac{1}{2}$-inch ribbon

- Thumbtacks
- Hair dryer or electric fan

 PROCEDURE

Part A

1. Place the plastic bags inside each other to form a triple-layered bag.
2. Put on the gloves. Now place the dry ice in the triple-layered bag. Crush it into relatively small pieces by hitting it gently with the hammer. It will crush easily, so little force is needed.
3. Still wearing the gloves, hold the bag from the bottom and have your partner add the dirt and cola.
4. Squeeze the bottom of the bag to mix the ingredients as evenly as possible. Be careful not to squeeze the bag or pull on it so hard that it tears.
5. Your partner should now add the water. **Immediately** begin squeezing the bag to pack the material down as if you are making a snowball (which you are!). Keep working the mixture in the bag until it solidifies into one lump. This is your comet.
6. Wearing the gloves, carefully remove the comet from the bag and place it on the newspaper.
7. Observe your comet for the rest of the class period. Record your observations in the Data Collection and Analysis section.

Part B

Remember that the Sun is the source of the energy that makes a comet visible. Because the Sun's radiation is always flowing outward, the material in the tail of a comet is pushed outward, away from the Sun.

1. Using the thumbtacks, attach one end of each ribbon to the same place on the Styrofoam ball. This is your model comet with a tail.
2. Standing to the side, hold the comet about 2 feet from the hair dryer or fan. Have your partner turn on the hair dryer or fan blowing toward the comet. If using a hair dryer, make sure it is on the coolest and highest fan setting. Adjust the speed of the fan, or distance from the comet to the hair dryer or fan, until you see the comet's tail blowing outward.

(continued)

Comets: Dirty Snowballs *(continued)*

3. Now walk the comet around your partner in an elliptical path, moving in closer, and then moving away, as shown in Figure 2. Make sure that your partner always directs the hair dryer or fan toward the comet.

4. Record your observations below in the Data Collection and Analysis section.

Figure 2

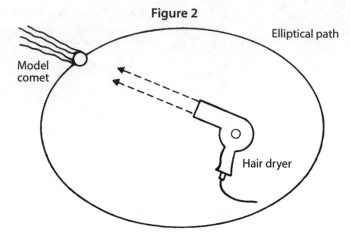

DATA COLLECTION AND ANALYSIS

Part A

1. Describe the appearance of the comet when it was first removed from the bag.

_____

2. Describe any changes in the comet during the course of the class period.

_____

Part B

Record the behavior of the tail as the comet moves along its orbit around the fan.

_____

CONCLUDING QUESTIONS

Part A

1. How was the appearance of the comet different at the end of the class than it was just after you made it? Give reasons for any changes you observed.

_____

_____

(continued)

Comets: Dirty Snowballs *(continued)*

2. Relate your observations of the changes in the comet during the class period to the lifetimes of real comets. In particular, consider what happens to a comet each time it nears the Sun.

_____

_____

Part B

How did the comet's tail behave as the comet proceeded around its orbit? Does the comet's tail always follow behind the head as the comet orbits?

_____

_____

EXTENSION

How does a comet tail's visibility depend on the relative position of the Earth, the Sun, and the comet when the comet is near its closest approach to the Sun? Think of the setup for Part B, and imagine yourself as the Earth, orbiting the Sun in a circle inside the comet's orbit. Describe the relative positions of the Earth, Sun, and comet that yield the best visibility from Earth. Do the same for worst visibility.

☀ Follow-up Activities ☀

Part A

1. When Comet Halley passed by in 1986, spacecraft from several countries were sent out to study it. Research the results obtained from these satellites, and present your work to the class.
2. Disaster movies have been made about the impact of a comet or asteroid on Earth. We have never seen such an impact on Earth firsthand. But, in 1994, Comet Shoemaker-Levy 9 collided with Jupiter, and was observed by the Hubble Space Telescope. Use the World Wide Web to learn about this impact.

EXTENSION

Relate the ingredients you used in making the comet with the actual composition of a real comet. How might you have made a more accurate model?

Part B

Find and examine images of as many comets as you can and compare the appearances of their tails, noting whether the dust tail or the ion tail, if either, is more prominent. Make a poster of comet pictures and present it to the class.

Looking for Life (In All the Right Places?)

 INSTRUCTIONAL OBJECTIVES

Students will be able to

- understand the organizational complexity of solar system exploration.
- describe some of the issues in undertaking a space mission to search for life.

 NATIONAL SCIENCE STANDARDS ADDRESSED

Students demonstrate an understanding of

- The impact of science, such as historical and contemporary contributions.
- interactions between science and society.

Students demonstrate scientific inquiry and problem-solving skills by

- using evidence from reliable sources.
- identifying variables.
- working in teams to collect and share information and ideas.

Students demonstrate effective scientific communication by

- arguing from evidence.
- using data to resolve disagreements.

 MATERIALS

For each subcommittee:

- Internet access, especially for the following suggested sites:

  http://spaceart.com/solar/eng/history.htm
  http://www.faqs.org/faqs/astronomy/faq/
    part6/preamble.html
  http://www.scibridge.sdsu.edu/coursemats/
    introsci/Solarsys/lecture.html
  http://argyre.colorado.edu/life/
    lifesolarsys.html
  http://unmuseum.mus.pa.us/lifess.htm
  http://pds.jpl.nasa.gov/planets/
  http://riceinfo.rice.edu/Fondren/Woodson/
    jsc-archive.html

  http://www.okbu.edu/academics/natsci/
    planet/links/solar.htm
  http://www.reston.com/astro/explore.html
  http://www.seds.org/nineplanets/nineplanets/
- A word processor and printer, or writing paper and pencils
- Chalkboard, whiteboard, or marker board

HELPFUL HINTS AND DISCUSSION

Time frame: Two periods
Structure: In three subcommittees
Location: In class, and wherever library and computer resources are

This activity may not be for everybody. You should judge whether or not your class is capable of the degree of cooperation required. This exercise is meant to give students a feel for the necessary background research and decision making that is a part of solar system exploration. The committee work is used as a framework to guide students in their limited research in three areas: the nature of life, the history of solar system exploration, and conditions around the solar system. Divide the class into three groups (subcommittees) for the first session. Try to ensure that each group contains a mix of high and low achievers. This activity should lead to spirited discussions, and even a bit of frustration on the part of some students as they struggle to work in committees. We strongly suggest that during the first session each subcommittee has access to at least one computer with Internet access, and preferably a word processor or text editor on the same computer so that they can write their reports as they go. During the sessions, you may help with organizing the committees, finding resources, and generating the reports. The subcommittees may be allowed to complete their reports outside of class, as long as they are done before the second classroom period.

SCORING RUBRIC

Due to the unique nature of this activity, and to reinforce the message that in certain real-world situations the team succeeds together, we suggest you give the class a collective, advisory only grade (not counted toward a student's final grade) on this activity. You may base this grade on your evaluation of the quality of their collaborative work as shown by the subcommittee reports and final recommendations. Extra credit (which *may* count toward a student's final grade) can be awarded to students who do the Follow-up Activity. The quiz can be scored from 1 to 4 correct.

ADAPTATIONS FOR HIGH AND LOW ACHIEVERS

High Achievers: Encourage these students to do the Follow-up Activity.

Low Achievers: No adaptations necessary.

INTERNET TIE-INS   See the Materials section.

QUIZ
1. Why does it seem likely that life might exist elsewhere in the universe?
2. How does space exploration differ from other science in the way it is carried out?
3. Why are we limited to the solar system for direct exploration for life?
4. What kinds of skills are needed to carry out solar system exploration?

Looking for Life (In All the Right Places?)

☼ BEFORE YOU BEGIN ☼

One of the most intriguing questions people ask is whether or not there is life anywhere else in the universe. Is life a rare occurrence, perhaps even unique to Earth? Or is it common, spread throughout the universe in many forms, whether we are able to detect it or not? There are billions of stars in our galaxy, and perhaps billions of galaxies in the universe. So even if life is fragile and hard to get started, it seems likely that some kind of life exists elsewhere in the universe.

To search for life around faraway stars, we can only use passive methods, like listening for accidental or intentional radio signals from civilizations with technology comparable to ours. But since the beginning of the Space Age, with the launch of *Sputnik* in 1957, we have at least the possibility of visiting some other places closer to home in the solar system where life may exist. Some missions whose goal was to look for life have already flown. Others will undoubtedly be undertaken in the coming decades.

Much of science is done the way you might think, by individual scientists or small teams working in laboratories of various kinds. But space exploration is a different matter. It takes thousands of people, huge amounts of money, and up to a decade or more to design, plan, and carry out a single significant planetary mission. It takes people with many different skills to run a planetary exploration program. These skills include not just math and science, but also engineering, manufacturing, and most importantly, organization and management. Sometimes, scientific progress depends more on a participant's ability to run a good meeting and to work well with diverse groups of people than it does on his or her ability to do a calculation or experiment.

MATERIALS

- Internet access, especially for the following suggested sites:
  http://spaceart.com/solar/eng/history.htm
  http://www.faqs.org/faqs/astronomy/faq/part6/preamble.html
  http://www.scibridge.sdsu.edu/coursemats/introsci/Solarsys/lecture.html
  http://argyre.colorado.edu/life/lifesolarsys.html
  http://unmuseum.mus.pa.us/lifess.htm
  http://pds.jpl.nasa.gov/planets/

  http://riceinfo.rice.edu/Fondren/Woodson/jsc-archive.html
  http://www.okbu.edu/academics/natsci/planet/links/solar.htm
  http://www.reston.com/astro/explore.html
  http://www.seds.org/nineplanets/nineplanets/
- A word processor and printer, or writing paper and pencils
- Chalkboard, whiteboard, or marker board

PROCEDURE

Your class will play the role of the NASA Mission Planning Committee (MPC). You have the responsibility to carry out Project Look-For-Life (LFL), a mission to determine if there is or ever has been life anywhere in the solar system other than on Earth. Because of budget cutbacks, you can only send one mission to one location in the solar system. To save money, the mission does not include astronauts and cannot return to Earth, but it can communicate by radio with NASA headquarters. Your recommendations are due at the end of the second classroom period.

(continued)

Looking for Life (In All the Right Places?) *(continued)*

During the first classroom period, and outside of class if necessary:

1. Your teacher will divide the MPC into three subcommittees. Each subcommittee must *organize itself* to accomplish the work described below. Use all resources available, including textbooks, the Internet (especially the sites listed in the Materials section), and libraries, to get the latest information for your report. Continue your research after the class period, if necessary. Each subcommittee will issue its results as a report, *no more than one page in length.* All members of each subcommittee should review and sign the document.

2. Subcommittee A will decide on an official definition of "life." This is not as easy as it sounds. What essential characteristics make one thing alive, while another without those characteristics is not? Include a discussion of the conditions (temperature, pressure, chemical environment, etc.) necessary for life. Your official document is to be entitled "Project LFL—Definition of Life."

3. Subcommittee B will review and summarize any two previous attempts to find evidence of current or past life in the solar system. Do not restrict yourself to space missions, and do not include searches for signals from beyond the solar system (like the SETI project). Describe where these missions looked, how they tested for life (visually, by chemical tests, etc.), their results, and how those attempts could have been improved. Your official document is to be entitled "Project LFL—Previous Attempts."

4. Subcommittee C will research and describe three places other than Earth where life might be found. Do not limit your possible locations to the surfaces of planets. Describe each of your three locations, including conditions of temperature, pressure, and chemical environment, as well as any existing evidence for or against life there. If unusual transportation methods (like boring 10 km into the sulfur surface of Io) are required, describe those. Your official document is to be entitled "Project LFL—Potential Targets."

During the second classroom period:

5. Appoint a timekeeper and stick to time limits.

6. Subcommittees A, B, and C will each designate a representative who will report their results to the full Mission Planning Committee. All members of the MPC are invited to comment on the reports. Limit this phase of the project to no more than 5 minutes per subcommittee, and stop at that time whether you are finished or not.

7. Armed with your official "Definition of Life," "Previous Attempts," and "Potential Targets" documents, work as a full committee to decide the single best place to go to find life. Use *only* the information in the three reports. Limit this phase of the project to no more than 10 minutes, and stop at that time whether you are finished or not.

8. Now that you have chosen a single target, work as a full committee to decide what scientific equipment must be sent on the mission. Don't worry about the rocket or communication or navigation systems. These are standard NASA equipment. Do include all equipment to check for life, and local transportation if needed. Limit this phase of the project to no more than 10 minutes, and stop at that time whether you are finished or not.

9. Together, as the full MPC committee, choose one student (the "representative student") who will spend no more than 5 minutes combining the results of steps 7 and 8 into a very brief document, *no more than one paragraph in length,* entitled "Project LFL—Recommendations."

(continued)

Looking for Life (In All the Right Places?) *(continued)*

10. The representative should verbally present this document, along with printed or written copies of all four documents, to the powerful chairperson of the House Budget Committee (also known as your teacher) who will decide whether or not to finance this program.

   Tips for running a productive committee meeting:
   - Pick one person to lead the meeting.
   - Choose one person to keep notes of important points on a blackboard or sheet of paper.
   - Be respectful, and give each member a chance to speak.

CONCLUDING QUESTIONS

1. How did you feel about working in committees? What problems did you encounter getting the work done?

   _____

   _____

   _____

2. Do you agree with the final target and type of mission chosen by the MPC? Why or why not?

   _____

   _____

   _____

3. Which committee did you find more efficient, your subcommittee or the full MPC? Why do you think this is so?

   _____

   _____

   _____

☼ Follow-up Activity ☼

The explosion of the space shuttle *Challenger* in 1986 is a case in which NASA's committee-based process for making decisions failed. Research and write a brief report on the *Challenger* disaster. Include the causes of the accident, and any lessons learned and changes in procedures that NASA made as a result.

Planets Around Other Stars!

 INSTRUCTIONAL OBJECTIVES

Students will be able to
- describe how discoveries of extra-solar planetary systems are being made.
- compare the properties of extra-solar planets with planets in our solar system.

 NATIONAL SCIENCE STANDARDS ADDRESSED

Students demonstrate an understanding of
- the evolution of the solar system.

Students demonstrate scientific inquiry and problem-solving skills by
- identifying variables in nonexperimental settings.
- using evidence from reliable sources.

Students demonstrate effective scientific communication by
- arguing from evidence and data.

 MATERIALS

For each group of two or three students:
- Access to the World Wide Web
- Calculator

HELPFUL HINTS AND DISCUSSION

Time frame: 40 minutes, or a single period
Structure: In groups of two or three students
Location: In class

Groups of students will work together to search the World Wide Web for information about planets discovered around other stars. They can start at the Web site shown under Internet Tie-ins. This site lists many other interesting extra-solar planet Web sites that the students can use to do the activity.

ADAPTATIONS FOR HIGH AND LOW ACHIEVERS

High Achievers: Encourage these students to look more deeply into the methods of detecting extra-solar planets. They can research the Doppler Shift, which is the principle behind the wavelength-shift method described in the Before You Begin section. They can also look into the "wobble" method of detection. Some of the links on the indicated Web sites have more detailed explanations of these methods. High achievers should also be encouraged to do the Extension and Follow-up Activity.

Low Achievers: Have reference materials available that students can consult as they work. You can pair low achievers with high achievers for this exercise.

SCORING RUBRIC

Full credit can be given to students who correctly describe the extra-solar planets found around the stars in Table 1. Extra credit can be given to students who do the Extension or Follow-up Activity. The quiz can be scored from 1 to 4 correct.

  INTERNET TIE-INS   http://www.seds.org/nineplanets/nineplanets/other.html

QUIZ
1. What do we mean by an "extra-solar planet"?
2. Why is it hard to detect these planets directly?
3. How does Newton's First Law help us search for extra-solar planets?
4. Why would the presence of liquid water be an especially important discovery on an extra-solar planet?

Planets Around Other Stars!

☼ BEFORE YOU BEGIN ☼

Since the time astronomers learned that Earth is just one of a family of planets orbiting the Sun, a fairly typical star, it has been natural to speculate whether there might be planets orbiting around other stars. The vast distances between Earth and even the nearest stars, plus the small size and faintness of a planet compared to a star, make it extremely difficult to detect these objects, called **extra-solar planets**. Only in the last several years have scientists developed observational methods that have revealed planets in orbit around other stars.

Two of the best of these methods rely on Newton's First Law, which says that a body will move along a straight path at a constant speed unless an external force acts on it. So, if a body is observed to move along a curved path, or if its speed changes, then it must be acted on by an external force. The source of that force, we conclude, is the gravitational tug from an orbiting planet, which may be too small and faint to see directly.

The first of these methods looks for "wobbles" in a star's motion as it moves through space. The amount of wobbling can tell astronomers how much mass the planet has and how big its orbit is.

The second method searches for variations in a star's speed. We can observe how fast a star is approaching Earth or moving away from Earth by studying how wavelengths of light from the star are shifted from their normal values. These shifts depend on the star's speed. It's like listening to the pitch of a train whistle. To the engineer on the train, the whistle's pitch is constant. But if the train is approaching you, the whistle's pitch sounds higher than normal. If the train is moving away from you, the pitch sounds lower than normal. The amount of the shift you hear indicates how fast the train is moving. This effect is called the **Doppler Shift**. For a star moving at a constant speed on a straight path, the amount of the shift will remain constant. But if a star has a shift that *changes,* the amount and timing of the change can tell how much mass an orbiting planet has and how big its orbit is.

It is interesting to think about whether extra-solar planets might be able to support life as we know it on Earth. Among many other things, the planet would need to have liquid water, and the star couldn't be too hot or too cool. A very hot star would emit too much ultraviolet light that would be harmful to life. A very cool star wouldn't provide enough energy to support life.

In this activity, you will search the World Wide Web for information about extra-solar planets and the stars they orbit.

✂ MATERIALS

- Access to the World Wide Web
- Calculator

(continued)

Planets Around Other Stars! *(continued)*

 PROCEDURE

1. Log onto the following Web site:
   http://www.seds.org/nineplanets/nineplanets/other.html
   You will see some information about the discovery of extra-solar planets. At the bottom of the page there is a list of links. Explore those links to find information about planets discovered around the stars listed in Table 1 in the Data Collection and Analysis section.

2. Find information about each planet's mass and fill in the appropriate values in Table 1. The mass of a planet is sometimes given in units of Earth masses (M_E), and sometimes in units of Jupiter masses (M_J). Table 1 asks for the mass in Jupiter masses. To convert a mass given in Earth masses to a mass in Jupiter masses, divide by 318.

3. The semimajor axis of a planet's orbit is its average distance from the star. Find each planet's orbital semimajor axis and fill in the appropriate values in Table 1. The units are normally given in astronomical units (AU). One AU is the semimajor axis of the Earth's orbit around the Sun.

4. See what other interesting information you can find about these planets, and enter it in Table 1. Subjects might be the date of discovery of the planet; whether the planet's estimated temperature would allow liquid water; distance of the star from our solar system, etc.

 DATA COLLECTION AND ANALYSIS

Table 1

Star	Planet Mass (M_J)	Orbital Semimajor Axis (AU)	Interesting Findings
51 Pegasi			
55 Cancri			
HD 114762			
70 Virginis			
16 Cygni B			
14 Herculis, also called Gliese 614			

(continued)

Planets Around Other Stars! *(continued)*

❓ CONCLUDING QUESTIONS

1. Which planet in Table 1 orbits closest to its star? _____

   Which orbits farthest? _____

2. Which is the most massive planet? _____

   Which is the least massive? _____

3. Are any of these planets similar to Earth in mass? How many times more massive than Earth is the least massive planet in Table 1?

   _____

   _____

4. What can you conclude about the likelihood of discovering a planet of Earth's mass with the methods used to find the planets in Table 1?

   _____

   _____

EXTENSION

There are several stars that seem to be surrounded by disks of dust and gas that might eventually form planets. Among these are Beta Pictoris, a star about 50 light-years away. Go to http://oposite.stsci.edu/pubinfo/pr/96/02.html and then write a paragraph about this star and its disk.

☀ **Follow-up Activity** ☀

There are several research programs in progress and some new ones being proposed to search for extra-solar planets. Some of these are listed in the links to the Web site for this activity. Choose one program and write a research article about it, including the method of detection, the kind of stars being observed, and results, if any.

Science Series: Our Solar System

WALCH PUBLISHING

Share Your Bright Ideas

We want to hear from you!

Your name_____Date_____

School name_____

School address_____

City _____State _____Zip_____Phone number (_____)_____

Grade level(s) taught_____Subject area(s) taught_____

Where did you purchase this publication?_____

In what month do you purchase a majority of your supplements?_____

What moneys were used to purchase this product?

____School supplemental budget   ____Federal/state funding   ____Personal

Please "grade" this Walch publication in the following areas:

	A	B	C	D
Quality of service you received when purchasing	A	B	C	D
Ease of use	A	B	C	D
Quality of content	A	B	C	D
Page layout	A	B	C	D
Organization of material	A	B	C	D
Suitability for grade level	A	B	C	D
Instructional value	A	B	C	D

COMMENTS:_____

_____

What specific supplemental materials would help you meet your current—or future—instructional needs?

_____

Have you used other Walch publications? If so, which ones?_____

May we use your comments in upcoming communications?   ____Yes   ____No

Please **FAX** this completed form to **888-991-5755**, or mail it to

   Customer Service, Walch Publishing, P. O. Box 658, Portland, ME 04104-0658

We will send you a **FREE GIFT** in appreciation of your feedback. **THANK YOU!**